# Piggy Ban.

*This Book is Really About love of Life And love of Family*

*5% (Repairs made)*

*Enhances your quality of Life And Reduces your Financial stress*

***Piggy Bank Your Home*** is not a substitute for legal, accounting or other professional advice. You should always proceed with caution. This book is your beginning point.

PIGGY BANK YOUR HOME, 2nd edition

PUBLISHED BY DH MEDIA
In association with CoGrow Systems, Inc.

Contact: info@DennisHaber.com or voicemail: 516.822.1020

Additional copies may be purchased through
www.PiggyBankYourHome.com

All names mentioned in this book are composites of the many
hundreds of clients Dennis Haber has personally helped find a
better way. Any similarity of names and events to living persons
is purely coincidental.

Cover and page design by Stephen Looney.
Authored by Dennis Haber.
Edited by Vikram Rajan.

ISBN 978-0-9797022-0-4

# *Praises for* Piggy Bank Your Home™

Rarely have I met a person with a true commitment to the betterment of people in need. Dennis Haber transcends his role as educator and author. He has replaced need with solution, despair with hope. This book unlocks a treasure chest for anyone who wants to retain their home and to seize every beautiful moment. Many of my clients have availed themselves of reverse mortgages. They have lived the rest of their lives with far fewer concerns and with a myriad of opportunities.

**- Beverly J. Bell, Esq., Partner**
**Humes & Wagner, LLP**

Reverse mortgages, as with most financial decisions, are something that should not be taken lightly and should not be rushed into. You should always discuss such matters with a professional trusted advisor. *Piggy Bank Your Home* is a great place to learn about reverse mortgages and to begin the process to determine if it is right for you.

**- Peter E. Buell, CPA, Tax Partner**
**Marcum & Kliegman, LLP**

Each section of *Piggy Bank Your Home* provides the reader with a different way to become familiar with the program. I have been in the reverse mortgage business since 1989 and I truly feel every loan officer who works with seniors should carry one of these books with them.

**- Roger Cresswell, National Wholesale Manager**
**Financial Heritage**

Dennis Haber is passionate about enriching the lives of seniors. This book is a testament to that.

**- Vicki Ellner, Founder**
**Senior Umbrella Network (Brooklyn)**

*Piggy Bank Your Home* is an excellent resource tool. It is essential reading for attorneys, accountants and financial planners who advise their clients about reverse mortgages. The book is extremely informative, yet easy and fun to read.

**- Ronald Fatoullah, Esq., CELA, Principal/Founder**
**Ronald Fatoullah & Associates**

Dennis is one of the most knowledgeable, caring people in the reverse mortgage industry. His expertise and sincere concern for his clients is evident in *Piggy Bank Your Home*.

**- Neil B Garfinkel, Esq., Partner**
**Abrams Garfinkel Margolis Bergson, LLP**

Dennis offers an easy-to-digest look at the world of reverse mortgages. With discussions of risk reversal, eligibility requirements, out-of-pocket costs, *Piggy Back Your Home* is a handy reference for anyone seeking to navigate their way through the complexities of reverse mortgages.

The book explains such basic issues as the difference between a forward mortgage and a reverse mortgage, the changing face of reverse mortgages, and when is the right time for a reverse mortgage. Dennis writes in a straightforward, conversational tone, and offers many easy to follow illustrations, and appropriate cautions.

**- Jack Halpern, CEO**
**My Elder Advocate**

Under the appropriate circumstances, a reverse mortgage can be a godsend. Dennis Haber is one of the most knowledgeable persons I have encountered in the industry.

**- Robert J. Kurre, Esq., CELA, Managing Attorney**
**Robert J Kurre & Associates P.C.**

This is a brilliant, much-needed book. Its simplicity makes it required reading for all those who are curious about the reverse mortgage program.

**- Megan Lawler, President**
**Baydocs, Inc.**

As director of business development for The Health & Business Alliance, I have seen Dennis Haber position himself as the go-to guy for 'Everything you wanted to know about Reverse Mortgages, but were afraid to ask'. Dennis is the ultimate resource for reverse mortgages. As baby boomers and their parents age, his sage advice and counsel can provide the key to unlocking the wealth trapped in one's home.

**- Steven D. Lichtenstein, Director of Business Development**
**The Health & Business Alliance**

*Piggy Bank Your Home* is an easy-to-read balanced analysis of the widely misunderstood concept of Home Equity Conversion Mortgages. While Mr. Haber acknowledges that a reverse mortgage is not appropriate for everyone, he explains how today's more flexible programs can play an important role in the retirement planning for many seniors. In my opinion, *Piggy Bank You Home* should be required reading for anyone interested in learning more about a reverse mortgage.

**- Don J. Mariani, President**
**Senior Resources Network, Inc.**

At last, a book that gives a comprehensive overview of reverse mortgages! Dennis Haber, in one book, sheds light on a product that so few really understand and so many can benefit from. This book works for anyone and everyone who is concerned about funding their retirement years. Unlike all the books I have read regarding reverse mortgages, finally we now have the ultimate reference of reverse mortgage information. Thanks Dennis!

**- Mario Martirano, President/Founder**
**Agency for Consumer Equity Mortgages, Inc.**

Dennis Haber has created a thorough, readable, and well organized text on this very important and emotionally-charged issue. Financial service professionals have to help their clients separate fact from myth. *Piggy Bank Your Home* is a perfect way to accomplish this. I have added this book to my office library and I intend to refer to it often as more people need creative ways to accomplish their life goals.

**- Sam Miller, President**
**Society of Financial Service Professionals (Nassau Chapter)**

My excitement over this book is dual focused: As Executive Director of the Queens Medical Society I applaud this book, which empowers the elderly to maintain independence and control over their lives. As a Licensed Clinical Social Worker, I appreciate the sense of hope and optimism it imparts to seniors.

**- Janine Regosin, L.C.S.W., Executive Director**
**The Medical Society of the County of Queens**

*Piggy Bank Your Home,* clearly falls into the unique category of a MUST READ. Just as conventional wisdom dictates that you have a fire extinguisher and smoke detector in your home even though you may never have a fire, having and READING *Piggy Bank Your Home* will provide the same comfort.

Knowing that you have options, that you know the right questions to ask and qualified and caring people to consult with will provide you or people you care about with a sense of comfort and security.

- **Dan Schaefer, Ph.D, President**
**Peak Performance Strategies**

Dennis Haber is one of the most honorable professionals in the reverse mortgage industry today. His pioneering work in the state of New York has helped so many seniors reclaim their financial independence and dignity. *Piggy Bank Your Home* will do the same for seniors all across the country. His highly principled caring approach combined with his unmatched work ethic has earned him the moniker, the "reverse mortgage man." It is indeed an honor to call him a friend and to have him as a colleague.

- **Charles Seelinger, Jr., CEO**
**Senior Funding Group**

Dennis Haber has concisely and expertly explained a unique financing strategy (reverse mortgages) which will become an even more important planning tool with the sub-prime debacle. There are many older people who have too much pride to ask their children for money. Reverse mortgages could provide the solution. Bravo Dennis on behalf of us old timers.

- **Frederick Smithline, Esq., Counsel**
**Eaton & Van Winkle, LLP**

Dennis Haber brings his vast experience not only in the field of reverse mortgages but as an attorney to this outstanding book. He provides seniors and their families with the information that they need to make an important decision. It may be the best way to maintain their dignity, independence, and remain in the homes they love, and in the communities they helped build.

- **Steven H. Stern, Esq., CELA, Partner**
**Davidow Davidow Siegel & Stern, LLP**

*Piggy Bank Your Home* is an excellent reflection of Dennis' enthusiasm for the reverse mortgage industry. I encourage all of my peers to get a copy of this very informative and enlightening book.

**- Sal J. Turano, President**
**Abstracts, Incorporated**

*Piggy Bank Your Home* gives you a clear and concise understanding of the reverse mortgage program. All too often, we have heard the old saying, "All our money is in bricks." The bricks can provide you with the joy of a secure retirement and financial independence. *Piggy Bank Your Home* is a "must book" for all to read.

**- H. Joseph Watts, Former Vice President**
**Council of Senior Centers and Services of New York**

........................................

## *Dedication*

This book is dedicated to my clients who have experienced the life changing power of reverse mortgages and who have fallen in love with their futures again.

........................................

Start Living And FALL in love
w/ your Life Again - And
let Good oak help lead
the Way

# Table of Contents

# Foreword

Dennis Haber's book *Piggy Bank Your Home* is positively creative, pioneering, cutting edge and visionary. I say these things because this book is an expression of his desire to ensure that we make right decisions. This book will amaze you because of the depth of the information it contains about reverse mortgages.

I am an entertainer. Always have been and always will be. I sing and do comedy. I made some bold moves in my lifetime. Imagine working with Harry Belafonte, Eartha Kitt, Alan King, Hoagy Carmichael, Johnny Carson and Ed Sullivan, just to name a few. Not bad for a girl from Boston, Massachusetts.

You see, I believe that all of us can accomplish anything we want to, providing we take action. Wishing something to happen will not make it happen. Hoping something will change will not make it so. You must empower yourself! I'm going to let you in on a little secret I learned many years ago: I learned that each of us has the power to effectuate change in our lives. If you don't think that you have this power, then remember this, "I Helen Halpin McCarney do hereby grant you the power to change your life."

Everyone involved with Ms. Senior America knows about this power. This organization is made up of special ladies who recognize that our best years are still in front of us. And I bet that your best years are also in front of you. (This also applies to the guys-you have to tell them everything.)

Let me tell you a quick story: My friend walked up to me one day and said, "Helen, (she called me Helen probably because it's my name), I think you will make a great contestant in the Ms. New York Senior America pageant." She continued to tell me about the pageant. I became intrigued. I told another friend that I was thinking about entering the pageant. Her response floored me. She said, "Helen, it's a big risk. You may not win." Well, not only did I win the Ms. New York Senior America crown, I also won the nationals and became Ms. Senior America 2005.

The point is this: I had given myself the power to act. I did not let my fear defeat me. And do not let your fear of making a wrong decision stop you from considering an option that may be right for you.

In my travels, as Ms. Senior America, I have talked to many of my peers all across this great country. Many seniors today are not enjoying the American Dream of a peaceful and happy retirement. The culprit is usually not enough money.

I know a number of people who have had the courage to act... the courage to take those beginning steps. The power they granted themselves changed their lives forever. They went out and got a reverse mortgage. Their American Dream was restored.

We know that no program is right for everyone. It is up to you to investigate the positives and negatives of the program. This book will help you examine this and so much more.

On behalf of seniors all across America, I thank Dennis Haber for writing this easy to read book.

May your next years be your best years!

**- Helen Halpin McCarney**
**Ms. Senior America 2005**

# Preface

For many of us, the phrase "planning for long term care" is a new concept and unfortunately, one that is given very little attention as we try to meet the demands of our day-day-routine. All too often, in my line of work as the CEO for the Alzheimer's Association Long Island, families come to us when they are at crisis point and their number one concern is, "How is my Mom or Dad going to pay for the long-term care that will be needed now that they've been diagnosed with Alzheimer's disease?" Keep in mind that when we look at a long-term illness, we are talking an average of twelve to fifteen years. And midway through the process, finances often run out.

Unfortunately, with all levels of government looking to push more and more long-term care services back into the community, families are finding it increasingly difficult to finance the cost of long-term care for a family member who is ill. Given the fact that nursing home fees range anywhere from $10,000 to $15,000 a month and the cost of in-home help is extraordinary, it is no wonder why families are struggling to finance this needed care.

While my primary work is focused on families coping with dementia and/or Alzheimer's disease, in reality, illness can strike anyone at any time. And the daunting task of providing long-term care for a loved one is an issue that many of us will face as baby boomers begin to age.

But there is help. Dennis speaks to these issues in this wonderfully simple, user-friendly book. Piggy Bank Your Home is a tool that anyone can use to get quick intelligent answers to difficult questions. After reading this book, it became exceedingly clear to me that everyone needs a plan, and that planning should take place as early as possible so that all available resources can be uncovered to ensure the highest quality of care while avoiding premature placement into an institution.

For some, the equity in a home just might be the key to obtaining a secure financial future as we live out our golden years, but as with everything there are pitfalls. In this book, Mr. Haber takes an in-depth and objective look at many issues of concern and provides comprehensive, but understandable answers for his readers.

Piggy Bank Your Home is a must read for everyone and I look forward to sharing this book with many of my clients, helping them to navigate the world of a reverse mortgage and making their golden years all that they hoped for.

**- Mary Ann Malack-Ragona, Executive Director & CEO**
**Alzheimer's Association Long Island**

# Introduction

It has often been said that a picture paints a thousand words. In *Piggy Bank Your Home*, the illustrations help you visualize what your tomorrow could be like. Imagine casting off all money issues and focusing on those things that give you the most pleasure. Perhaps it is traveling, or spending time with the grandkids, or rediscovering that hobby long ago forgotten. Or perhaps it is taking total control over the endless stream of bills. Whatever it is, this book allows you to dream again.

An equally important goal is to take the fear out of the process. These illustrations will help you grasp important reverse mortgage concepts. This book is a wonderful way to make the acquaintance of an outstanding mortgage program that could make a huge difference in your life. Imagine having a personal, easy to understand guide that will get you through the process. You can avoid the pitfalls more easily with this book.

We urge you to consider all of your options. Getting a reverse mortgage is like a parachute jump: You have to get it right the first time. This book will act as your very own parachute, ensuring a soft and successful landing.

The key to a better tomorrow starts with asking good questions today. This seminal work also contains the many key questions that you must ask. However, you may have other original questions begging for an answer. One tool to help you formulate these other questions is to think of bringing six friends with you: Who, What, When, Where, Why & How.

Before you can think in terms of what COULD be possible, you will have to select good and competent people to be on your team. You will need a first rate reverse mortgage originator. Depending on your comfort level, you may also wish to seek advice from other professionals.

More and more professionals are becoming familiar with the program because their clients are demanding answers. This book also provides a way for the busy professional to help educate clients that yearn for a thorough yet simple and complete explanation about how reverse mortgages work. In fact, it is critical that clients become aware of their options. Thus reverse mortgage knowledge becomes another arrow in the professional's financial advice quiver.

This book and my work with our elders is a labor of love. This statement is not, by any means a bromide. You see, many of our elders today have a feeling of helplessness. Often they do not know where to turn. I know that feeling and it is my life's goal to ameliorate the financial turmoil our elder's face daily. Many years ago, when I was in law school, a headache became the harbinger of a serious and potentially debilitating illness. The resulting evanescent paralysis caused me to make a pact with my maker. I promised myself that I would do something special with my life, if I survived the brain surgery. I am convinced, that helping seniors regain their dignity and independence is that special something, I was meant to do. I have changed many lives. I hope to do the same for you.

A reverse mortgage could help you fall in love with your future again. It will make the next years of your life the best years of your life. This book is really a story about love of life and love of family.

But before we begin, you must first understand just how important the reverse mortgage has become for seniors across the United States. The balance of this section will address this salient point.

A long time ago, many of our today's seniors were our country's heroes. During WWII and the Korean War, they sacrificed much for love of country. At first America remembered and responded. Many of our gallant men and women received a college education under the GI bill. Many became homeowners because of the ubiquitous VA & FHA loan programs. Our warriors, returning to civilian life, prospered. And so did America. Many years later, something sinister and ominous took hold. Those in power became afflicted with "historical dementia." They forgot about those that did so much. Those once young warriors, are now experiencing the decrepitude that accompanies longevity. Our seniors once again need America to remember and respond. But it is a different America today. Our past heroes have become victims of circumstance, as big business lobbyists have overrun Washington (and our state capitals). "We the people" has lost its meaning as corporate America has become the new master to serve.

A new war is being waged in this country. It is a war against this country's most precious resource- our elders. Our past heroes, including those who fought in Vietnam, have become the "enemy." Congress has made it more difficult for seniors to declare bankruptcy, even though 50 per cent of all bankruptcies are due to health related issues; even though the credit card companies can still entice seniors to obtain more cards with billions- yes that is billions- of unwanted solicitations, knowing that seniors couldn't make the payments on the additional credit given.

Congress has made Medicaid planning a minefield, under the Deficit Reduction Act. Congress has caused seniors untold anxiety by the passage of the program known as Medicare Part D, which is making the insurance and pharmaceutical companies rich. Many states are in fiscal crisis, and the universal remedy and protocol has been to increase property taxes. Accordingly, our fixed income seniors are extremely vulnerable, as this "scorch the earth" policy has become the typical reflex.

In this new war, the weapon of choice for our seniors has become the reverse mortgage. This book will arm seniors and their families with the tools to fight and win back their independence and their dignity. Our elders will be able to protect the family dynamics. Many care-giving children will no longer have to quit their jobs or forego promotions because they have to care for mom and/or dad.

Our heroes will not have to choose between having heat in the winter or air conditioning in the summer, as they ration their meager savings. Our warriors will not have to limit the meals they will eat in a day, or eat cat or dog food because it is all that they can afford. Our protectors of liberty will not have to have their electricity shut off because they need to use the money to buy medication.

The new battleground has literally shifted to the front doors of our elders. And they now have one weapon that will help them reclaim their future. However, the bigger battle is to make "We the people" have meaning once again. Unfortunately, that will take a little longer.


- Dennis Haber, Esq.
Long Island, NY

# ARE YOU FEELING THIS WAY TODAY?

FINANCIAL INSECURITY

DEPRESSION

ANXIETY/STRESS

# THIS COULD BE
# YOU TOMORROW.

FINANCIAL FREEDOM

EMOTIONAL SECURITY

PEACE OF MIND

# HOW DO YOU GET
# FROM HERE

# TO HERE?

# ANSWER:
### Maybe It's Time To Consider
# A Reverse Mortgage.

## WITH IT

Suddenly you have financial independence, dignity, and peace of mind. You can rewrite the story of your life...and live happily ever after.

## WITHOUT IT

You will continue to struggle with your finances. You will always be counting your pennies.

# KILL 2 BIRDS
# WITH 1 STONE.

1. Get access to funds
2. Keep ownership of home

## BEST OF ALL WORLDS

GET MONEY

•

STAY IN YOUR HOME

•

NEVER MAKE A MONTHLY
MORTGAGE PAYMENT

# YOU MUST TAKE ACTION:

You must enter into a
"**partnership**" with your home.

Condos and Co-ops too!

A Reverse Mortgage is the tool you can use to **quickly** and **easily** draw money out of your primary residence.

You now have the power to change your life and do the things you want to do.

# THINK OF YOUR HOUSE AS A PIGGY BANK.

Filled with money just waiting for you to get at it.

Your house is a piggy bank because over the years the value has grown, creating wealth!

1950's To The Present

Your house may have increased in value 1000%, 2000%, 3000%, or more since you purchased it.

# VERY LITTLE COMES OUT OF YOUR POCKET

Not only will a Reverse Mortgage enable you to remove money from your home and put it into your pockets... Your home will also pay most of the costs associated with obtaining a Reverse Mortgage.

Your out of
pocket costs

Your pocket with a
Reverse Mortgage

> The house is keeping its part of
> your partnership agreement:
> # DOING ALL THE WORK

1. Appreciating in value.

2. Acting as your personal piggy bank.

3. Paying for your Reverse Mortgage Investment, (expenses).

4. Putting money in your pockets so you can live your hopes and dreams.

Relaxing and enjoying life is easy with a Reverse Mortgage. The possibilities are endless. You are limited only by your imagination.

Go on vacations

Fix up the house

Pay bills without stress or worry

Give money to children/grandchildren in need

Purchase a home

(Proprietary program)

Your home is returning its love by providing untapped equity to make your life **BETTER!**

# A REVERSE MORTGAGE CAN PROTECT YOU FROM THE FINANCIAL STORMS OF LIFE.

## Without a Reverse Mortgage

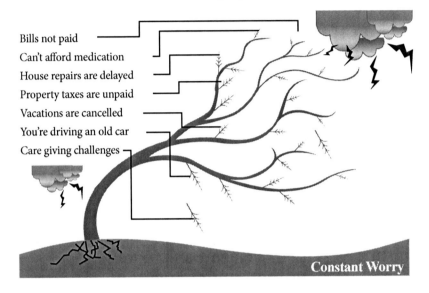

Bills not paid
Can't afford medication
House repairs are delayed
Property taxes are unpaid
Vacations are cancelled
You're driving an old car
Care giving challenges

**Constant Worry**

## With a Reverse Mortgage

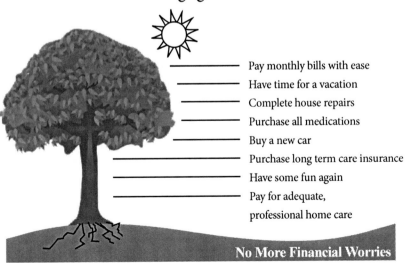

Pay monthly bills with ease
Have time for a vacation
Complete house repairs
Purchase all medications
Buy a new car
Purchase long term care insurance
Have some fun again
Pay for adequate,
professional home care

**No More Financial Worries**

# Learn *The NAME GAME*

Federal Housing Administration:  FHA

Housing & Urban Development:  HUD

Home Equity Conversion Mortgage:  HECM

When you see or hear FHA, HUD, or HECM, know that the United States Government is guaranteeing the loan. They are referring to the same Government insured reverse mortgage loan program.

# Proprietary Program

A proprietary program, private label or "private brand" program are innovative programs not guaranteed by the government. These programs usually provide financing options for seniors living in more affluent areas.

# RISK REVERSAL

*You can stop the process after signing the application documents without incurring a financial penalty!*

## BEST OF ALL WORLDS

Federal law provides you with a 3-day waiting period after closing. You have the right to change your mind even after you sign all the closing documents... *

### *-Without incurring a financial penalty-*

*REGULATION Z - TRUTH IN LENDING ACT - 12CFR226.23

# WHY IT'S A GOOD TIME TO CONSIDER
# A REVERSE MORTGAGE

Dollar
benefits
are up

Number
of new
programs
on the rise

Interest
rates
are down

Closing costs
are going
down
(Some programs)

FHA/HECM closing costs will generally range from 5 - 12% of the benefit amount.

Now you can live "happily ever after."

# TAKE YOUR TIME

Consider ALL the facts & ALL your options

FINISH LINE

## Some Options You May Consider

1. Sell your home and move into a rental apartment.
2. Sell your home and move into a less costly home.
3. Sell your home and move in with family.
4. Sell your home and move into an assisted living community.
5. Liquidate assets to obtain cash.
6. Obtain a community governmental grant for home repairs.
7. Obtain a conventional mortgage.
8. Enter nursing home.

# ELIGIBILITY REQUIREMENTS

· Must own Your Home ·  ✓
· Must Be 62 Or Older (all owners) ·  ✓
· Must Be Your Primary Residence ·  ✓

## Suitability Appropriateness
Some things to consider. This list is not all inclusive.

1. Time you intend to stay in your home.  ✓
2. Budget constraints require increase in cash flow.  ✓
3. Need to eliminate high interest credit card debt.  ✓
4. Plan to avert bankruptcy/foreclosure.  ✓
5. Provide for adequate home care.  ✓
6. Provide gifts to heirs in need.  ✓
7. Remodel home to fit health needs.  ✓
8. Enough proceeds to pay off current mortgages/liens (see page 25).  ✓
9. Avoid liquidating invested assets.  ✓
10. Create new financial and estate plan.

**ONLY YOU CAN DETERMINE WHETHER A REVERSE MORTGAGE IS WORTH PURSUING!**

Life saver for adult children who can't provide financial aid to parents because they are taking care of their own family.

•

No income, asset, or credit requirements.

•

No personal liability.

•

No monthly mortgage payments to make.

•

No prepayment penalty.

•

The interest accrues only on the money that you actually take.

•

Flexible options to obtain money.

•

Tap into your equity today and remain in your home.

# DISADVANTAGES

Monthly payments you receive are not indexed to inflation.

•

Interest is compounded over time.

•

Closing costs incurred.

•

Debt rises while equity decreases.

*Consider this:*

Remember when you purchased your home? You evaluated the positives and negatives, the plusses and minuses, and the advantages and disadvantages. Just think of the incredible opportunity that would have been lost if you just focused on the negatives, the minuses and the disadvantages. Similarly, when exploring whether to obtain a reverse mortgage, attention must be given to both sides.

Because the amount you receive each month can be increased AND because you do not make monthly mortgage payments AND because no one can tell you what a reverse mortgage is worth to you - ALWAYS consider the disadvantages together with the advantages. Only then will the entire picture be in focus. Reverse mortgages are allowing seniors all across the country to remain in the home they love.

# WHY PEOPLE CHOOSE TO GET A REVERSE MORTGAGE

## *Could this be you or someone you know?*

Veronica
**88 years old**
After paying off a huge mortgage had over $100,000. It kept her in the home well into her nineties.

Leroy
**77 years old**
Only wanted to spend his time painting and wanted to stop taking money from his brother.

Victor
**83 years old**
Paid off $60,000 in tax liens as well as $80,000 in judgments.

Shelley
**86 years old**
Paid for 24/7 home care.

Joan
**86 years old**
Paid off a $300,000 mortgage her late husband took out to save a troubled business and put money in her pocket to fix up her house.

Virginia
**91 years old**
Was able to stay in her home. Her daughter made sure she got the reverse mortgage before she ran out of money.

William
**75 years old**
Sold his out of state home and used the profit to purchase a home in the suburbs. He then reimbursed himself for most of his outlay with a reverse mortgage.

Helen
**63 years old**
Received peace of mind, as she utilized the line of credit option to create a forced "savings account" that will grow tax free. (Her credit limit was merely increasing.) She intends to retire in 4 years.

Patricia
**71 years old**
Gave a gift to her 2 children and 4 grandchildren and had plenty of money left over for herself.

Peter
**72 years old**
Couldn't wait to get the reverse mortgage because he wanted to purchase a new car.

Wanda
**69 years old**
Took a load off her shoulders when she paid off her mortgage and $30,000 in credit card debt.

Phyllis
**65 years old**
Booked a trip to Europe. This was the promise she had made to herself.

Ralph
**79 years old**
Paid for a college fund for his 2 grandchildren.

Mary
**77 years old**
Refurbished her 30 year old kitchen and put in a new bathroom with some of the proceeds from her reverse mortgage.

Barbara
**71 years old**
Stopped a mortgage foreclosure, and paid off property tax liens.
She had enough money left over to supplement her monthly shortfall.

........................................................................................................

**You are limited only by your imagination as to
what you can accomplish with your reverse mortgage.**

*"It ain't what you don't know that gets you into trouble. It's what you know for sure that just ain't so."*

- Mark Twain

## Here are some *untrue* statements that many believe to be true.

- You will make a monthly mortgage payment.
- The lender will own your home.
- The lender can force you to leave anytime.
- Your heirs are personally responsible for paying the loan back.
- It is just for "poor" seniors.
- Your reverse mortgage proceeds adversly affects Social Security and Medicare benefits.
- It is a government scam.
- You must be in good health to qualify.
- You have personal liability on this loan.

Remember: All these statements are UNTRUE. You probably have heard other untrue statements as well.

23

Don't let someone who knows
nothing about the program
TAKE YOUR DREAMS AWAY!

Friend or family member         You

**It's like cooking a meal,** take 3 ingredients and throw them into a pot. Boil for 3 minutes and instead of a meal you get dollars.

## Important points

- *The older you are, the more money you can get.*
*(Age of youngest borrower if 2 or more people own the home)*
- *The value of your home will help to determine how much you can get (depending on program guidelines).*
-*The higher the expected interest rate (FHA), the lower the dollar benefit will be. The lower the expected interest rate (FHA), subject to the monthly adjustable floor limit, the higher the dollar benefit will be.*

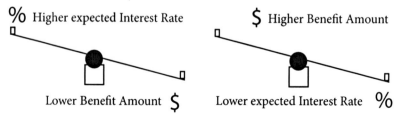

# A REVERSE MORTGAGE LOAN BECOMES DUE WHEN:

---

## House Is Sold

---

---

## No Longer Your Primary Residence

---

---

## Death*

---

\* Death of surviving borrower

# BASIC WAYS TO ACCESS YOUR MONEY

## LINE OF CREDIT (LOC)

Take as much or as little as you need, when you need it. The reverse mortgage line of credit is different in that the amount contained in the line of credit has a built-in growth factor. The balance increases each month.
(Your credit limit is actually increasing.)

## TENURE

Receive an automatic monthly payment that will continue as long as the home is being used as your primary residence. This amount will continue even if you outlive your life expectancy.

## MODIFIED TENURE

Receive a smaller automatic monthly payment that is also combined with a Line of Credit option.

## TERM

Receive an amount greater than a tenure payment. This amount will last for a finite period of time. The automatic monthly payment stops after this time period is reached.

## MODIFIED TERM

Receive a smaller term amount combined with a line of credit.

## INITIAL DRAW

Receive an amount of your choosing combined with one of the noted payment plans.

## TOTAL WITHDRAWAL

Take all the funds in one draw.

### LINE OF CREDIT (LOC)

# $204,000

# TAKE WHEN YOU NEED

### TENURE

## $1,000 PER MONTH

JAN ⟶ DEC· ·➤

### MODIFIED TENURE
## $600 PER MONTH

 +

$105,000 LOC    JAN ⟶ DEC· ·➤

### TERM

## $2,500 PER MONTH FOR FIXED TIME PERIOD

JAN ⟶ DEC· ·➤ **STOP**

### MODIFIED TERM

## $2,000 PER MONTH FOR FIXED TIME PERIOD

 +

$40,000 LOC    JAN ⟶ DEC· ·➤ **STOP**

### INITIAL DRAW

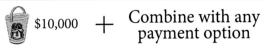 $10,000 + Combine with any payment option

***\* Term Portion of Payment Stops at a point in time.(There are no more buckets of money.)
Talk to your expert reverse mortgage loan officer or advisor to discover how long your term payments will last.***

# It is your job to get answers to your questions.

Many people tell me that they do not know what questions to ask. I have provided you with a list of 52 questions that will get you the information that you will need. Also, think of your own questions to ask.

## YOU WILL THEN BE READY TO MAKE YOUR DECISION.

1. What other options are available to me?
2. Are there any options that I have not yet considered?
3. Do I really really trust the potential reverse mortgage originator I am about to choose?
4. Why should I choose this person to be on my team?
5. What are the 3 biggest reasons the reverse mortgage program works for me?
6. What are the differences in the various reverse mortgage programs?
7. Which one is right for me?
8. What determines how much money I can receive?
9. What are the different ways I can receive the funds?
10. Are there any restrictions on the use of the funds?
11. How long will the money last?
12. Who should I consult with about obtaining a reverse mortgage?
13. People say so many inconsistent things about reverse mortgages. Who should I believe?
14. What are the more common misconceptions about the program?
15. Can I get a reverse mortgage if my children own the home?
16. Why does my local banker know so little about the program?
17. My local banker wants me to get a traditional loan instead. What should I do?
18. Must I be in good health in order to qualify for a reverse mortgage?
19. Are the reverse mortgage proceeds taxable as income?
20. Why is a reverse mortgage a good financial & estate planning tool?
21. When does the loan have to get paid back in full?
22. If I owe more than the home is worth, what liability do I or my family have?
23. What role does competency play in getting a reverse mortgage?
24. If I own a condominium unit or a cooperative apartment can I get a reverse mortgage?
25. Are there any situations that would prevent me from getting a reverse mortgage?

26. How long does the whole process take?
27. What responsibilities do I have to the lender once I get the reverse mortgage?
28. Is there a pre payment penalty?
29. If I own two homes, can I get a reverse mortgage on each?
30. Will a reverse mortgage interfere with Medicaid planning?
31. Can a reverse mortgage be used to compliment Medicaid planning?
32. Why is independent third party counseling mandated?
33. What is this counseling all about?
34. Are there any situations where this counseling can be waived?
35. Can my counselor tell me how to take the money?
36. Can the counselor demand that I use a particular company and/or originator?
37. If I am of reverse mortgage age and my spouse is not, can we both still qualify for a reverse mortgage?
38. Can I ever lose title to my home after obtaining the reverse mortgage?
39. Can I get the reverse mortgage if the house needs repairs?
40. After my death, how much of the remaining equity will my children get?
41. I have a life estate in my home. My children have the remainder interest. Can I still qualify for a reverse mortgage?
42. Are there special reverse mortgage requirements when I have a life estate?
43. My home is technically owned by a trust. Can I get a reverse mortgage?
44. Are there special requirements when title is held by a trust?
45. What are the closing costs for getting a reverse mortgage?
46. Who pays these costs?
47. How much are the out of pocket expenses?
48. After beginning the application process, what penalties will I face should I change my mind?
49. How costly is it?
50. Can I change my mind after I sign the closing documents?
51. Can the interest rate ever be locked in?
52. I own an expensive home, is there a different kind of reverse mortgage for me?

---

**Answers to these question can be found in Part 2.**

## My Questions To You

**DO YOU UNDERSTAND THE PROGRAM?**
**DO YOU HAVE QUESTIONS THAT HAVE NOT BEEN ANSWERED?**
**HAVE YOU CONSIDERED ALL YOUR OPTIONS?**

**The most important decision you will make once you begin the reverse mortgage process is in your selection of your reverse mortgage company & loan officer.**

All reverse mortgage companies are not the same.

All reverse mortgage loan officers are not the same.

Like everything in life, there is the good, the bad and the indifferent.

You would rather choose a good reverse mortgage loan officer over one that is bad.

You would rather choose a competent reverse mortgage loan officer over an incompetent one.

You would rather choose an honest reverse mortgage loan officer over one that is dishonest.

Your choice needs to know everything about the reverse mortgage process and programs.

1. Aging trends in this country
2. Care giving needs of seniors
3. Illnesses that affect ADLs (Activities of daily living, like eating, bathing dressing, etc.)
4. Chronic illnesses common to an aging population
5. Long term care issues
6. Social Security program
7. Medicare program
8. Medicaid program
9. Resource of professionals
10. Advance Directives (includes power of attorney, etc.)

# 5 Key Ways To Protect Yourself

1. Always be suspicious.
2. Involve other people in the decision making process.
3. Ask lots of questions.
4. Take your time in making this decision.
5. In the end make sure your decision is not based on the mere opinion of another. *Most important.*

*If it Feels Right - Trust your intuition -*
*If it Feels Right go for it*

# WITH YOUR REVERSE MORTGAGE
## YOU WILL EXPERIENCE!

1. A new lease on life.

2. Never financially depend on children or family again.

3. Retain independence and dignity.

4. Have money in your pockets.

5. Do all the things you have only *Start Living Fully —* thought about doing.

## BEHIND THE SCENES

Professional processing and underwriting ensures that you will receive your money at the earliest possible moment.

A team of caring service providers work hard to get you to the closing table.

# LOOK FORWARD TO

1. Never making another mortgage payment.

2. No personal liability
   on the loan.

3. Qualifying easily.

4. Always being in control.

5. Assisting adult children
   and/or grandchildren in need.

"WIN - WIN"
FOR PARENTS AND CHILDREN.

## TOTALLY AFFORDABLE

# ONE LAST THOUGHT

Think what your life will continue to be
like if you do nothing.

Think what your life will continue to be like
with more money in your pockets.

# THE CHOICE IS YOURS!

# PART 2:
# Answers To Questions From Pages 29 and 30

*The answers to these questions are concise by design. Detailed and complete answers would fill many pages. These questions illustrate the point that hiring a competent loan officer (loan originator) is like a parachute jump. You have to get it right the first time. This person is responsible for giving you information and for providing you with the answers to your questions. Choosing the right person is a very critical decision.*

*Imagine what would happen if you chose the wrong doctor or the wrong lawyer: Consequences will always flow from your bad decision. These answers are designed to give you some of the pieces to the reverse mortgage puzzle. Your loan officer (loan originator) will have to provide you with the remaining pieces. Therefore, it is up to you to pick the best available person.*

*These answers are for didactic purposes only. You should always consult with a qualified professional who will take your specific situation and goals into account.*

---

### 1 What other options are available to me?

Broadly speaking, you can sell your home or get a conventional mortgage. There are many opportunities here. Sell and move in with family. Sell and buy a more manageable home. Sell and move into an assisted living community. You get the idea. On the other hand, you can stay and obtain a traditional loan. These loans require that you make monthly mortgage payments. Before you make a decision, go slowly, get advice from professionals and talk to family. Many seniors have been taken advantage of by unscrupulous real estate brokers and unsavory mortgage professionals.

### 2 Are there any options that I have not yet considered?

Once you come to a conclusion ask yourself the above question. Then ask yourself if there are any questions that I should have asked but have not yet asked.

### 3 Do I really, really trust the reverse mortgage originator I am about to choose?

Notice that "really" is repeated. You must be convinced that this individual is not treating you as a mere customer so that he/she can sell you something. Because when some one "sells," they will tell you anything to get you to "buy." Rather, you would prefer to work with a person that has your best interest at heart. This person cares that you do the right thing....even if it means choosing an option other than a reverse mortgage.

### 4 Why should I choose this person to be on my team?

First you must like them. That individual must be likeable and pleasant. Then you must trust them. This means that they must have character and competence. Not only must they be honest, but they must be extremely competent. They must know their stuff. And the company they work for must be a member of the National Reverse Mortgage Lenders Association (NRMLA). As you proceed through these questions you will see just how important "knowing your stuff" becomes.

### 5 What are the three biggest reasons the reverse mortgage program works for me?

There are many reasons why this program may work for you. In fact it is changing lives all across the country. Typically this program will enable you to stay in the home and in your community. It provides you with the wherewithal to pay your bills with ease. It provides you with renewed independence and dignity that will help you fall in love with your future again. Simply put, the money issues are taken off the table. Everyone has their own reasons for obtaining their reverse mortgage.

### 6 What are the differences in the various reverse mortgage programs?

What you need to know is that there are differences among the programs. Let's split them up into two major categories: Government insured programs and non-government insured programs. The government insured programs are the FHA reverse mortgage programs, also referred by the acronym HECM (Home Equity Conversion Mortgage). They come in different varieties: Adjustable and fixed rate. Usually under the fixed rate program you will have access to less money than you would if you chose the adjustable feature. Also, at the time of this writing, you have only one option. You must take all the money in one lump sum. Different indices can also be used.

The adjustable variety will adjust monthly or annually. The margins will vary. The lower the margin the more money you will get. Under the adjustable feature you will have many options for choosing how to receive the funds. The government insured programs guarantee that you will receive your money in a timely manner.

The non-government insured loans are called private brand or proprietary reverse mortgage programs. They also come in the fixed rate and adjustable rate variety. These programs work best for high value homes because they do not cap (except for the FNMA Home Keeper program) how much of the home value will be counted. Because these programs are not insured, it is critical that you work with reputable and financially-secure lenders, mortgage bankers, and mortgage brokers.

### 7 Which one is right for me?

The answer to this question will depend upon your circumstances and what you wish to accomplish. For example, if you have a rather high existing mortgage balance, (where most of the reverse mortgage proceeds will go toward payment of that balance), it may be desirable to take a fixed rate program. Remember this is the program that requires that all the money be taken in one single payment. On the other hand, if you are looking to use the reverse mortgage line of credit or receive a monthly payment, you may be better off with the adjustable loan. This is why you must hire the most competent person available. They will be able to explain in detail which program will better meet your needs.

### 8 What determines how much money I can receive?

Usually there are three things that will be determinative on this question. The age of the youngest borrower, the value of the home (up to a limit under some programs) and the interest rates (under the FHA program it is called the Expected Interest Rate). These things taken together give you a number called the Principal Limit. The older the youngest borrower is, the lower the interest rate is, and the higher the value is (except for some programs) the greater your Principal Limit will be.

### 9 What are the different ways I can receive the funds?

Under the FHA/HECM program, there are 5 different ways to receive the funds: Tenure, Term, Line of credit, Lump sum and Partial lump sum. Think of a monthly tenure payment as a bucket of money that will never go empty. The payment will last as long as you are using the home as your primary residence.

A term payment is higher than a tenure payment; however the term payment will stop at some point in time. Think of this monthly payment as a bucket of money that will be empty at a point in time.

You will get these payments (tenure & term) automatically each month.

When the line of credit option is chosen, you can access money when you want it. Under this option you must request the funds in order to receive it. It will not automatically be paid to you each month.

You can receive all the money in one payment or you can take out an initial (smaller) lump sum. You can even combine the aforementioned methods (except if you take all the money in one payment). As circumstances change, you can revise how you receive the funds.

**10** **Are there any restrictions on the use of the funds?**

There is no one looking over your shoulders. You can spend the money any way you see fit.

**11** **How long will the money last?**

The twin goals of the program are 1) for you to do what you need and want to do and 2) to make the money last as long as possible. Therefore you must treat the reverse mortgage proceeds with the utmost respect. The line of credit option, even with the principal limit growth factor built in, will last until you spend the balance in the line of credit. The term payment will last until the term of years has expired.

Depending on your circumstances, the monthly amount needed could last a relatively short time to many many years. You will need to talk to your loan officer about this. A tenure option will last as long as a borrower is using the home as a primary residence. Depending upon your needs, this is the option that is referred to when it is said that there is a plan that you can not outlive. You may also want to discuss this with your counselor when you have the counseling session.

**12** **Who should I consult with about obtaining a reverse mortgage?**

Ideally you may want to ask an attorney, accountant, financial planner, or some other professional, if you have access to such professionals. If you do not have such access, then you need to do research, get comfortable with the program and take your time. If you talk to family or friends it is important that they know a lot about the program. Imagine the results if in fact the reverse mortgage was a perfect option and you were talked out of it because the professional or friend or family member you relied upon did not know much about the program!

On the other hand, you must always ask questions. Why is it not for me? What other options do I have? And why am I better off with the other option? The final choice is yours to make. Remember years from now the person that you listened to may no longer be part of your life.

**13** **People say so many inconsistent things about reverse mortgages. Who should I believe?**

The main reason you will hear inconsistent thoughts are because there are many misconceptions about the program. They sadly get repeated as if they are facts. It is exactly because of this that you need to come to your own conclusion. Talk to people that have already obtained the reverse mortgage. Ask questions. Lots of questions. I keep saying this because you can not relinquish your responsibility. And you must find that loan originator who is thoroughly knowledgeable about the program and senior issues. Take your time. This is not a sprint. Treat the reverse mortgage process as a marathon. It takes a lot of training and conditioning. Never proceed unless and until you are confident about the program and about the loan officer you picked. Also never wait until you are in dire financial straits. Whenever possible plan ahead.

**14** **What are the more common misconceptions about the program?**

Many people believe if they get the reverse mortgage the bank will own the home. The bank will never own the home. You will never give up title as a result of getting a reverse mortgage.

Many people believe that you still have to make monthly mortgage payments to the lender. You know that this is never the case. Monthly payments are never required to be made.

Many people believe that the loan becomes due when the first borrower passes away. This is not true. It becomes due when the survivor passes away.

Many people believe that a reverse mortgage is only for those seniors that are poor. Nothing can be further from the truth. Seniors in every income bracket are discovering the benefits that reverse mortgages have to offer. Your research will uncover other misconceptions.

**15** **Can I get a reverse mortgage if my children own the home?**

If title is out of your name and in the name of your children, you will not be eligible for the program. If your children agree, they can place the title to the home back in your name. There may also be tax implications as well. Seek out the advice of an elder law attorney. You also better hope that no

41

judgments or liens have attached to the property during the time your children owned the home. See question 41.

**16** **Why does my local banker know so little about the program?**

The reason for this is because your banker makes more money selling conventional mortgages. Also the bank knows that it would be an incredible task to train all their mortgage originators to sell reverse mortgages. So when you walk into your bank, your banker wants you to get a "traditional" mortgage. You may be discouraged from looking into the benefits of a reverse mortgage.

**17** **My local banker wants me to get a traditional loan instead. What should I do?**

Never forget that you have the power to say "no." So many seniors have gotten themselves into trouble because they really do not have the ability to make those monthly mortgage payments. They take some of the proceeds from the loan, put it aside TO MAKE THE MONTHLY PAYMENTS.

When the money is used up, they can no longer make the payments. Imagine that this happened to you. When you can no longer make the payments, you run the risk of the bank foreclosing. I do not think this is what you bargained for. With the melt down of the Alt-A and subprime programs, a reverse mortgage becomes a more realistic option.

**18** **Must I be in good health in order to qualify for a reverse mortgage?**

Health is never an issue. The loan is not medically underwritten. In fact, many people get the reverse mortgage because they need care in the home.

**19** **Are the reverse mortgage proceeds taxable as income?**

A lot of the reverse mortgage advertising says, "Get tax-free income." It is really not income. You are using equity in the home.

If you invest the reverse mortgage proceeds, you could be converting generally non taxable proceeds into taxable proceeds. However, it's recommended that you speak with a tax advisor.

**20** Why is a reverse mortgage a good financial and estate planning tool?

Many seniors are literally sitting on a gold mine. The program could convert the "gold" into a lifetime of cash. The program enhances your quality of life and reduces your financial stress. It allows you to reshape and retool your financial plan because it gives you a respite from worrying how those bills will be paid.

If you live in a high value home and are able to take advantage of the proprietary program you may want to consider estate tax planning. The additional amount of proceeds you can tap into will enable you to purchase additional life insurance that will further protect your family.

**21** When does the loan have to get paid back in full?

The loan becomes due upon the happening of a maturity event. A maturity event occurs when you sell the home; the home is no longer a primary residence of either borrower (assuming 2 people own the home), or upon the death of the survivor.

**22** If I owe more than the home is worth, what liability do I or my family have?

A reverse mortgage is a non-recourse loan. This means that there is no personal liability to you, your heirs, or to your estate (to pay the loan back). The value of the house upon sale is the only thing the lender can look toward to pay the loan back. If you have money in a bank account for instance, the lender can not get at those funds.

**23** What role does competency play in getting a reverse mortgage?

As in any legal transaction, the parties must be competent to act on their own behalf. However, if there is an issue of incompetence, then it is important to have a durable power of attorney in place. If such a document has not been timely executed, then you will have to resort to the courts. This option is costly and time consuming.

**24** If I own a condominium unit or a cooperative apartment can I get a reverse mortgage?

You can get a reverse mortgage if you own a condominium unit. Until FHA allows a reverse mortgage on a cooperative apartment, it can be done under some proprietary programs. At this time those programs are limited to certain jurisdictions with high concentrations of co-ops. Talk with your loan officer to discover if this particular program is available in your area.

### 25 Are there any situations that would prevent me from getting a reverse mortgage?

You may be prevented from getting a reverse mortgage whenever your existing loan balance is greater than the amount you can realize from your reverse mortgage. The net proceeds from the program first have to pay off this balance. (And/or the balance of other liens). Title issues may preclude you from getting to the closing table. Defaults and claims made on any federal loan may be another reason that you may not be able to complete the transaction (FHA/HECM reverse mortgage).

There are basically three eligibility requirements: All borrowers must be 62; all must "own" the home; it must be a primary residence.

### 26 How long does the whole process take?

The process should take anywhere from 3 to 6 weeks providing there are no unusual circumstances that need to be dealt with. Ask this question of your loan originator. Some companies are taking months. This is an indication they do not know what they are doing. You must choose wisely.

### 27 What responsibilities do I have to the lender once I get a reverse mortgage?

The responsibilities you have now are the responsibilities you will have when you obtain your reverse mortgage. You must pay your property taxes, keep the homeowners insurance in force and keep the home in good repair.

If you own a condo you must do the above and continue to make your monthly maintenance payments. In the case of a coop you must continue to make the maintenance payments and keep the unit in good repair.

### 28 Is there a pre-payment penalty?

There is never a pre-payment penalty on the FHA & Home Keeper reverse mortgage programs. Some proprietary programs may not accept a voluntary pre-payment if it occurs within a certain time of receiving the loan. You will need to speak with your loan originator.

**29** **If I own two homes can I get a reverse mortgage on each?**

No. The home must be a primary (principal) residence. You can only have one primary residence at a time.

**30** **Will a reverse mortgage interfere with Medicaid planning?**

If the proceeds are spent in the month that they are obtained, it will generally not interfere with Medicaid planning. If your loan originator does not know what you are talking about, you may want to reconsider your pick. However, each state has different rules so it is important that you check with an elder law attorney in your state. To locate one, go to www.NAELA.org. A good loan originator should also be able to direct you to an attorney that knows the rules for your state. *National Ass Elderly Lawyer*

**31** **Can a reverse mortgage be used to complement Medicaid planning?**

Yes. It can help you stay in your home by providing a resource to pay a caregiver over and above what Medicaid allow. For example, Medicaid may pay for 3 hours a day, when you need 10 hours a day care. You can use the proceeds to pay the difference. It is suggested that you speak with an elder law attorney. *wonderful safeguards*

**32** **Why is independent third-party counseling mandated?**

Counseling acts as a buffer. It insures that you are not being coerced into doing something you do not want to do and also contains an education component. Let's say you choose an originator who provides you with a bunch of wrong information. The counselor will be able to correct this misinformation. You will also want to look around for a new person to work with.

**33** **What is this counseling all about?**

Every counselor has a protocol that they must follow. This protocol is constantly evolving to insure that relevant information is exchanged. Among other things your counselor will discuss the reverse mortgage concepts, a budget, the affects of a negative amortization loan, identify your goals, etc. When there is a non-borrowing spouse, that person must also be counseled. Once you have the counseling you should have a feeling of confidence that you are doing the right thing. Hopefully your loan originator was able to engender this feeling as well.

**34** **Are there any situations where this counseling can be waived?**

Sometimes. When one refinances their existing reverse mortgage additional counseling can be waived in very limited circumstances.

**35** **Can my counselor tell me how to take the money?**

The counselor can only suggest. They can never tell or demand that you take a particular course of action.

**36** **Can the counselor demand that I use a particular company or originator?**

Absolutely not. Likewise the originator can not demand that you use a particular counselor.

**37** **If I am of reverse mortgage age and my spouse is not, and we both own the home, can we both still qualify for a reverse mortgage?**

Both of you must be of reverse mortgage age. Taking the underage party off title is rarely a good idea. The loan becomes due upon the death of the borrowing spouse. If the non-borrowing spouse does not have a source of funds to pay the loan back, then the sale of the home could be the only option available.

**38** **Can I ever lose title to the home after obtaining a reverse mortgage?**

No. You own the home today. You will own it after getting the reverse mortgage. Remember, you have certain obligations that you must keep. See questions 21 and 27.

**39** **Can I get a reverse mortgage if the house needs repairs?**

Generally this is not a major issue. Many repairs can be escrowed for. However, in those instances when the cost of repairs exceeds a certain amount, some repairs will have to be completed before the closing. If on the other hand, a substantial amount of repairs are required, you may be prevented from getting the reverse mortgage. Your loan originator should be able to guide you on this point.

**40** **After my death, how much of the remaining equity will my children get?**

This all depends on a variety of factors: How you accessed the money; longevity; interest rates; appreciation of the home. Usually there is equity left in the home.

**41** **I have a life estate in my home. My children hold the remainder interest. Can I still qualify for a reverse mortgage?**

Yes. The FHA/HECM program specifically permits this. The proprietary programs, having used the FHA/HECM program as a model allow this as well.

**42** **Are there special reverse mortgage requirements when I have a life estate?**

Because the children have an interest in the property, they must sign certain documents at the closing. If all the remainder interest parties can not make it to the closing, then a power of attorney could be used. However there is another thing that you must be aware of. Whenever title is transferred to another there is always a degree of risk. For example, if you transfer title to a child, while retaining a life estate and a judgment is obtained against that child that judgment could become a lien against that property. If a child gets divorced, then that property could become subject to that divorce proceeding. See Question 15.

**43** **My home is technically owned by a trust. Can I get a reverse mortgage?**

It depends whether the trust is inter vivos (created during your lifetime) or testamentary (takes effect upon your death). Most programs will not allow a testamentary trust. It also depends whether the trust is revocable or irrevocable. There is a general bias against allowing a reverse mortgage when title is in an irrevocable trust. A revocable trust is usually permitted. The specific trust terms are key and the lender has to agree to proceed. The lifetime beneficiaries of any trust can only be the borrowers and they must be of reverse mortgage age. A good loan originator, working with an elder law attorney, will be able to sort things out for you.

**44** **Are there special requirements when title is held by a trust?**

Among other things the trust must be an enforceable in your state; the trustee must have the power to encumber the property with a (reverse) mortgage; the beneficiaries (not the contingent beneficiaries) must be of reverse mortgage age; title to the property must be vested in the trust.

**45** **What are the closing costs for getting the reverse mortgage?**

The costs vary from program to program. Under the FHA/HECM program, mortgage insurance is required. This could add a substantial amount to your closing costs. However, you may make a mistake when you focus ONLY on the costs. The reason is that the costs notwithstanding, the reverse mortgage program could be the one program that winds up being the answer to your predicament. Discuss the costs and other options with your loan originator.

**46** **Who pays these costs?**

The costs are generally rolled into the loan amount. You will have the option to pay some of these costs out of pocket if you so choose. Some proprietary programs waive all the costs when you take all the money in one lump sum.

**47** **How much are the out of pocket expenses?**

You can usually roll the costs into the loan amount. However, you may wish to pay some of the fees out of your own pocket. The amount and type of fees vary in different parts of the country. Whether you choose to pay these fees directly is totally up to you. Such out of pocket costs may include an appraisal, termite inspection or underground oil tank testing. The FHA program usually no longer requires the termite inspection or underground oil tank testing unless the appraiser notices that a "condition" exists.

**48** **After beginning the application process, what penalties will I face should I change my mind?**

There are usually no penalties. Check the policy of the company that you employ. A good company will not charge you anything. Others will try to keep you in the deal by threatening that you will have to pay the appraisal, etc. Federal law says that should you exercise your right of rescission, you are entitled to get your appraisal fee back.

**49** **How costly is it?**

Please keep in mind that there is a huge difference between what something costs and what something is worth. The FHA/HECM program usually has a high cost because of the required mortgage insurance premium. You can review these expenses by viewing the Good Faith Estimate (GFE) document. Closing costs usually consist of origination fee, mortgage insurance premium (FHA/HECM), bank attorney fees, recording fees, title insurance charges, appraisal, credit report fees, etc.

However, never rely solely on this document as a means to pick the person and the company you will hire. For example a GFE with higher numbers may reflect reality. Whereas a GFE with lower numbers may be a ploy to get you thinking that if I choose company B, my closing costs will be lower Some proprietary programs have no costs should you take all the money in one lump sum.

Determining what your reverse mortgage is worth requires that you picture how different your life will be when you have access to these funds. You need to feel comfortable. If you think it is too expensive look at other options.

### 50 Can I change my mind after I sign the closing documents?

Yes. This is what the three day right of rescission is for. You will have three business days (Saturday is usually counted as a business day) to reconsider whether you wish to go through with your loan. Should you exercise this right, everything remains as if you never started the process.

### 51 Can the interest rate ever be locked in?

Under the FHA/HECM program, the expected interest rate, which helps determine the principal limit is locked at application. Being able to lock this interest rate at application is quite significant as it protects how much money you can get if the expected interest rate is higher at the time of your closing.

On the other hand, this lock in policy allows you to have access to more money if the expected interest is sufficiently lower at closing. Under the proprietary fixed-rate programs, the rate is usually locked a few days prior to closing. The FHA/HECM fixed-rate program also allows the principal limit to be protected at application.

### 52 I own an expensive home. Is there a different reverse mortgage program for me?

Yes. These are the proprietary programs that I have alluded to throughout these questions. These programs will usually provide greater proceeds than the FHA/HECM reverse mortgage.

# PART 3:
# Articles For Further Understanding

* The year in which each article was written (published) is noted at the beginning of each article. The varying content reflects the evolving nature of the reverse mortgage program. Some of the program features have changed and/or have been discontinued. The statistics, numbers, benefit amounts, interest rates, etc. noted in each article were accurate at the time the article was written. However, many of these figures change over time. Talk to a knowledgeable reverse mortgage specialist to obtain current rates, figures, and latest program features. Also, these articles have been re-edited & abridged from the original version.

# From Roosevelt's New Deal
# To The Deal of a Lifetime (2005)

Once again seniors are blazing new financial trails, this time with reverse mortgages. Just as contemporaries of the 1930s pioneered the concept of the thirty-year loan, today's seniors are pioneering the concept of reverse mortages. Before we tackle the subject of reverse mortgages, join me on a brief journey back in time.

In the early 1900's it was quite difficult for individuals to obtain mortgages. A down payment of 50% was usually required. The mortgage was typically a 5-year, interest only balloon mortgage.

The cataclysm of the Great Depression marked the end of unregulated mortgage banking in this country. Many home owners could not repay their debt nor refinance their existing loans. Banks lost the ability to lend when their depositors withdrew their funds.

Roosevelt's New Deal helped to restore the public's confidence in the mortgage banking industry. Soon the thirty-year amortized loan became available, along with standard interest rates and standard underwriting guidelines. Loans were securitized. This added liquidity to the mortgage financial markets.

Borrowers were doing things no one had done before. They were signing newly created documents that few people/professionals were familiar with. Today these very documents are considered "standard." Back then, borrowers were taking on 30 years of monthly payments. At that time, this was unheard of. Back then, a thirty-year loan was a vastly different concept. Today this is considered standard.

Back then the United States government insured these thirty-year loans. This was historic. Today this is standard. Years ago people were warned that they would lose their homes, that they would go broke if they signed these hard to understand mortgage documents. Imagine that.

Now let us fast forward to the present. There is a new financial concept that many seniors are now exploring. While reverse mortgages have been around since the early 1960's, they were unregulated and took on many forms and were called by different names. Relatively few were done. It wasn't until 1987 that Congress authorized the first government insured standardize reverse mortgage. Who says that history does not repeat itself? Now seniors are being asked to sign documents attorneys, accountants and financial planners have not seen before. Seniors are being told that if they get a reverse mortgage they will lose their home. Imagine that.

The bottom line is this: The thirty-year loan permitted today's seniors to raise their family in the home of their choosing. Together with many years of home value appreciation, another new type of financing (the reverse mortgage) is permitting these seniors to stay in their home AND live the life they were heretofore only dreaming about living.

Now it is time to weigh the facts. Just like the thirty-year mortgage changed the financial life for many of our ancestors, the reverse mortgage is doing the same for today's seniors, who are at least 62 years of age. In fact, the amount of seniors obtaining this financing is almost doubling each year. There are now competing reverse mortgage programs. This includes a special program for seniors that live in high-value homes.

Years from now, when we look back on the evolution of this product, people who remember will say, "What was the fuss all about?" It changes for the better, the lives of our senior citizens. Homes were saved from mortgage and tax-lien foreclosures. It enabled seniors to afford long-term care planning, home care and life insurance. It enabled seniors to accomplish estate planning goals. Because people are living longer, a reverse mortgage can provide financial peace of mind.

# A Short Primer on Reverse Mortgages: Things you Need to Know  (2002)

While reverse mortages are recognized in every state, relatively few seniors have taken advantage of its life changing features. The good news is that the abundant, powerful opportunities inherent in reverse mortgage financing are starting to be noticed by the seniors, their accountants, elder law and estate attorneys and financial planners.

This article will acquaint you with a vastly superior financial tool, your senior clients' should consider. It has the potential to make their lives measurably better. The first part of this article will discuss why a reverse mortgage should be a potent weapon in your clients' problem solving arsenal. The second part will tackle the specific features and requirements indigenous to reverse mortgages.

Join me on this brief journey of discovery, as I show you how you can truly make the lives of your clients happier and stress free by removing the financial worries that typically cause the "golden years" to turn into those "*olden* years."

A forward mortgage is the kind of loan you are familiar with. Monthly payments are made to a bank. As those payments are made, the unpaid principal decreases (amortizes), while the equity in the home continues to grow. With a reverse mortgage, the opposite occurs. The bank pays the borrower each month (if the borrower chooses this type of payment) while the equity in the home decreases.

The best news is that approval is not based upon a showing of specific income, liquid assets, nor a showing of credit worthiness. The only credit caveat is that judgments and liens must be paid at or before closing and any bankruptcy must be discharged. If a senior had to go through the typical underwriting process, many couldn't qualify for a forward mortgage. But they can qualify for a reverse mortgage!!!!!!!

In essence, when one chooses a reverse mortgage, a non performing, "dead" asset is transposed into a performing, "live" asset. The senior can unlock the equity that is just sitting there doing nothing. Because many seniors have difficulty qualifying for a loan, the equity could be tapped only by the sale of the home. Studies have shown, by overwhelming numbers, that seniors do not want to move. A reverse mortgage affords them the opportunity to remain in the home that they love.

A reverse mortgage has the pliability and flexibility to meet many needs of the senior borrower. For example, one reverse mortgage program permits title in a trust or a retained life estate (subject to review). The tax free proceeds can provide enough money to purchase a long term care policy, or other insurance. The funds can act as an emergency investment vehicle, estate planning device, or a retirement facilitator.

Thousands of our senior homeowners have a small mortgage balance remaining or no mortgage on their home. They may receive a pension and social security payments. Yet they still have dreams. Those dreams are unrealized because they struggle financially each month. Many seniors depend upon their children for financial help. The problem is that the children also have children of their own. Between trying to provide for their own retirement and attempting to put money away for their kids' college education, they are caught in a financial wedge. It is clear to see that a reverse mortgage can become a life saver for both families.

A reverse mortgage is unique because the loan does not have to be repaid until the home is sold, the senior dies, or permanently leaves the residence. No monthly payments are ever made by the senior borrower. At the time the loan becomes due and payable, the heirs can either choose to re-pay the loan and keep the house, or sell the home and keep the balance of the remaining equity. The choice is always theirs.

The amount one can receive depends on the age of the youngest borrower, the value of the home and the current interest rate. The minimum age requirement to obtain a reverse mortgage is 62. The age of the youngest borrower is used when there are two borrowers. It is important to remember, that the older the borrower is, the more money can be obtained. For example, assuming the same housing value, in the same community, a 75 year old can extract more equity than a 65 year old borrower.

The proceeds from a reverse mortgage can be received in a variety of ways. The borrower can choose a lump sum, or monthly payments for as long as they live in the home or monthly payments for a term of years, or a line of credit. They can even switch between payment options. Again, let me reiterate, that a reverse mortgage is very flexible.

The borrower has sole and total discretion when it comes to using the proceeds. Accordingly, seniors have used the proceeds to make needed home repairs, pay off credit card debt, judgments, mortgages and tax liens. Some have used the proceeds for home health care requirements. Others have purchased second homes, or traveled to their favorite places. The money can even be used to provide for a grandchild's college education. Some have even purchased different types of insurance policies. Remember, a fundamental purpose of the reverse mortgage is to allow seniors to dream again of a better life for themselves and for their family. It is important that they realize those dreams while maintaining their independence. A reverse mortgage accomplishes these feats.

A senior that obtains a reverse mortgage remains responsible for paying the property taxes, the homeowners insurance and must keep the house in good repair. The house must also be used as the primary residence.

Although the qualification process is easy, a reverse mortgage applicant must attend or receive reverse mortgage counseling from an approved HUD/FANNIE MAE/AARP counseling agency before the process can go forward. This is a good thing as it provides the seniors with additional information as well as possible alternatives to their situation. More importantly, it insures that the seniors are doing the right thing. I personally believe in getting family members together to discuss the situation. It is important that the entire family understand the benefits of this wonderful program.

Unfortunately, family and friends still promulgate wrong information about this program. Many people get into trouble not because of what they don't know. Rather they get into trouble because they rely on people who state "facts" as absolutely true that turn out to be just plain wrong. Sometimes, the attitude of family and friends will prevent those whose problems can be solved by obtaining a reverse mortgage, from going forward. It is a sorry sight to watch this happen. So watch out for people who appear to know what they are talking about.
So let's clear up these misconceptions once and for all. The following are the real facts.

 a. The borrower never makes a monthly payment.

 b. The borrower continues to own the home. The bank does not own the home.

 c. A reverse mortgage loan is a non recourse loan. This means that the heirs are not responsible for repaying the loan. In the event the sale proceeds do not cover the amount due on the mortgage, the bank has to accept this lesser payment as payment in full.

 d. The loan is not due and payable until the last surviving borrower dies, sells the home or leaves the residence.

 e. These benefits (Social Security & Medicare) are not affected by a reverse mortgage loan. Seniors in every economic strata and from all walks of life, are taking advantage of the benefits offered by reverse mortgages.

 f. Seniors can enjoy the cash flow that is created by reverse mortgages and they can still leave their home mortgage free to their children by combining guaranteed death benefit life insurance with the reverse mortgage. In the mean time, the seniors are living a life complete with dignity, while their children are relieved of the financial responsibility for their care.

g. Medicaid planning may not be appropriate in instances where the individual wants to maintain control over his/her assets. It is important to note that the government has been trying to restrict Medicaid eligibility for years. There is no guarantee that the program will remain viable in the future (see an elder law attorney before implementing Medicaid planning).

h. Unlike long-term care insurance, reverse mortgages are not medically underwritten. One of the most pressing issues & questions facing our growing senior population is how to effectively finance the out of control costs of long term care. A reverse mortgage can help accomplish this goal. These proceeds can be used either as the as the sole payment source for an aide or as a supplement to the hours received for home care benefits through Medicaid. For example, if Medicaid authorized twelve hours of care a day but the individual actually needs care twenty four hours a day to safely remain in the home, the proceeds of a reverse mortgage can be used to pay for the additional twelve hours of care a day. Taking into account all the reverse mortgage variables, a senior may very well be able to live their final years at home and avoid nursing home placement. This allows seniors to maintain their dignity and control over their long-term care.

i. A reverse mortgage is worth it. The costs are just one factor to look at. While the actual closing cost figures may be a little higher than typical FHA closing costs, it is important to remember that these costs can be financed. The main reason for this higher cost is that the HECM (Home Equity Conversion Mortgage) reverse mortgage plan requires mortgage insurance that is paid directly to the federal government. Also keep in mind that a senior is obtaining a loan that does not require income, asset or credit underwriting approval and they do not have to make monthly payments to a lender. Also keep in mind that other than selling the home, there is usually no other way to get access to this amount of funds. Question: If you had an opportunity to get a loan, with no personal liability and you didn't have to make a payment during your lifetime, would you consider it ? Well, this is an opportunity for seniors to regain their independence and dignity. When you focus only on closing costs and the TALC (similar to an APR-annual percentage rate), you are missing the bigger and more important picture. Only you can determine what a reverse mortgage is worth to you, taking into account its costs.

There are several distinct types of reverse mortgage loans. The most popular is FHA's HECM loan. This loan type comes in 2 varieties: the monthly adjustable and the yearly adjustable. The other loan type is Fannie Mae's Homkeeper loan. Generally this program is more conservative than the HECM. The third type of program is the "jumbo" reverse mortgage program. Under this program a senior can realize more from the equity.

It generally works when the home has an appraised value of $500,00 or more. Reverse mortgage loans are adjustable rate loans. Each type has different margins & caps. Only a small amount of institutions offer the jumbo program. Under the "jumbo" program, borrowers with high value homes can accomplish even more complex financial goals.

A reverse mortgage loan can only be made against a principal residence. FHA will make a loan against a 1-4 family unit, approved condo and PUDs. However, single family lending limits are used in 2-4 unit properties. Fannie Mae will only make loans against 1 unit properties only, approved condos & PUDs. A Reverse Mortgage is not currently available for co-ops.

Sometimes, repairs are required to be made on the home. Small repairs of $500 or less must be made prior to closing. Repairs greater than $500 but not exceeding 15% of the home value can be made can be made within six months of closing. Structural termite repair must be made prior to closing, while non structural repair should be completed within 90 days of closing.

The sole purpose of this article is to educate and debunk the misinformation that surrounds the exiting topic of reverse mortgages. This type of loan is safe. It allows our seniors to use the equity in their home to realize their dreams and possibly finance long term care, in such a manner which allows them to remain in the home.

# Co-ops and Reverse Mortgages Do Go Hand in Hand (2005)

Some co-op boards and attorneys representing same are reluctant to allow their tenant-shareholders to obtain a reverse mortgage. They wrongly apply a forward mortgage criteria and a forward mortgage mind set to such a request. This type of thinking is entirely inappropriate.

Before I debunk the usual arguments that are proffered, I first want to focus upon the fact, that as the years go by, more and more seniors will seek to get a reverse mortgage. For an individual that has already decided that they wish to remain in their home or co-op unit, a reverse mortgage will become a necessity. It will be the only way that a senior that is at least 62 years of age will be permitted to convert a portion of their equity into cash without selling and without making monthly mortgage payments.

Let us look at some of the brutal facts of reality. Consider this: In 1900 one in twenty five people were at least 65. Today one in eight have reached this milestone. In July of 1983, a startling thing occurred. For the first time in the history of the country the number of people 65 and over was greater than the number of teenagers. By the year 2050 there will be twice as many people in this category than teenagers.

Consider this: Both the birth rate and death rate are down. 20% of the baby boomers had no children. 25% had one child. For the past 30 plus years the birth rate couldn't surpass the death rate.

Consider this: According to the last census there were 35 million people in this country that have reached their 65th birthday. This number will double by the year 2030. Today this country has more people 65 or over than the entire population of Canada.

Consider this: No state has a senior population that exceeds 20%. In 20 years it is estimated than 30 states will have a senior population that exceeds this amount.

As this country's population continues to grow older many questions are raised regarding senior finances. Seniors are outliving their liquid funds. Social Security only takes one so far. Pensions are not measuring up. Close to 100,000 seniors a year are filing for bankruptcy. The dwindling return on investments is forcing seniors, our most precious resource, to tap into their principal. This quickly becomes a death spiral. Soon the only asset they have left is their home. This is the problem that co-op boards should be concerned about. The question then becomes: When a tenant shareholder is faced with a fixed income at a time of rapidly spiraling costs, how can they afford to continue to pay their monthly maintenance fees?

Every tenant shareholder should be allowed to obtain a reverse mortgage because of the following:
1) It is a non recourse loan.
2) No monthly mortgage payments will be made.
  (This means that a reverse mortgage is better than any other type of loan. The co-op is concerned that a tenant shareholder will not be able to make those monthly maintenance payments when the monthly mortgage payments are too high. This would be understandable for those forward mortgage loans. It is not understandable for a reverse mortgage loan because there are no monthly payments to be made).
3) Currently a special proprietary reverse mortgage program is limited to co-ops in New York. There is no reverse mortgage program for co-ops in any other state. Take advantage of this incredible opportunity.
4) This recognition agreement offers the same level of protection.

There is no need to look at a client's financials because they will never make those monthly mortgage payments. Our seniors today also have an opportunity to make their lives better. They have an opportunity through the use of a reverse mortgage to realize their hopes and dreams. Every co-op board should be embracing this incredible financial tool. Any co-op board that refuses to allow their tenant shareholder to obtain a reverse mortgage should reconsider because they do not have all the facts.

# Reverse Mortgages:
## A Concept Whose Time Has Come (2006)

Over the past few years, the number of seniors that are using this FHA/HECM program has doubled. In the not too distant future more of the major financial institutions will be offering this program. This general overview will help you understand this country's shifting senior demographics. It will also permit you to show your senior clients how they can unlock tremendous home wealth while staying in their home. This article will enable you to be among the first in your community to talk to your clients about a program many of your colleagues have heretofore ignored. Should they continue to ignore it, they will do so at their own financial peril. A Reverse mortgage will provide you with another "arrow in your client information quiver." Today, seniors want to know about all their financial options.

A confluence of forces have come together to place reverse mortgages directly in the limelight. The National Governors Association, CMS (The Centers for Medicare and Medicaid Services) and The National Council On Aging view reverse mortgages as an important financial and economic tool that is both helpful to our senior community and helpful to the federal, state and local government as well. Rebalancing this country's long term care system together with addressing the fear of impoverishment are important considerations.

Today seniors are sitting on over 2 trillion dollars worth of equity that represents over 950 million dollars in funds that could be made available from that home equity. CMS and the National Governors Association believe that Home Equity should be made available to off set the long term care costs and other medical expenses that would otherwise be paid by Medicaid.

Accordingly, we begin this article with a discussion of the negative voices professional advisors are using to dissuade their senior clients from going forward. After acquainting you with the basic concepts inherent in all reverse mortgage programs, we will review an actual case, using various scenarios. This will help you understand how much your client can realize under the various programs.

The bottom line is this: Conventional financing and the thirty year loan permitted seniors to raise their family in the home of their choosing. Together with many years of value appreciation, the reverse mortgage is permitting many seniors to stay in their home AND live the life they were heretofore only dreaming about living.

Some professionals today will echo the negative refrain of their colleagues of years ago. Seniors will be told not to go through with the reverse mortgage because it is a scam, too good to be true. Yes a reverse mortgage is different. It certainly is not a scam nor is it too good to be true. The government is insuring the majority of reverse mortgage loans.

Some professionals today are saying that the closing costs are too high. Their inquiry stops at the closing cost issue. This is a huge mistake many professionals are making. If a client wants to stay in the home and cannot qualify for a conventional loan or chooses not to obtain one, a reverse mortgage is the perfect tool.

The closing costs can be financed. Another way to look at this is that the equity of the house is paying the closing costs. Should the senior wish to they can pay the appraisal fee and other small fees (for example, termite inspection, etc.) if any, out of pocket. This means that for relatively small amount of out of pocket costs they can create a stream of money they can activate in a variety of ways, stay in their home and make their dreams come true while never worrying about making those monthly mortgage payments. On top of all this the government is assuring every senior that they will receive every penny they are due, even if the lender goes out of business. In other words, they do not have to worry about their reverse mortgage bank closing their doors. So if you focus upon the closing costs only you and the client will be missing the bigger more important picture.

Some professionals today are saying that the monthly payments are not indexed for inflation. Therefore don't get one. While the individual payments are not automatically indexed for inflation, it must be noted that the principal limit and the line of credit contain a growth factor that provides much more money over the life of the loan than if the client took the entire amount in one lump sum. You will never find this feature in any  other kind of loan product. If you or your client obtained a home equity line of credit from your neighborhood bank for $100,000 that was not accessed for 2 years how much would the line of credit be worth after this 2 year period? The answer is the same $100,000. Your line of credit would not grow. However, a reverse mortgage line of credit would be worth much more than $100,000 under this scenario. Under the FHA/HECM program, the line of credit will grow at 50 basis points above the note rate.

Some professionals today are saying that a reverse mortgage is a bad idea because the parent can not leave the home mortgage free to their children. Sometimes the parent(s) makes the same argument. In this case, all one can do is walk away. A parent will not obtain a reverse mortgage when they feel it is their obligation to leave their major asset to their children.

On the other hand, many parents believe that the home is the only financial vehicle that will protect them from their current financial storm. Leaving the home mortgage free to their kids is not the focal point. The financial and mental well being of your client is. While seniors know that money is not the most important thing, they also know that the lack of money affects everything that is important.

In order to figure out how much your client can receive from a FHA/HECM reverse mortgage you must know a few things about your client and their situation. We will focus on the FHA/HECM reverse mortgage because that makes up 92% of the reverse mortgage market. Three things are used to determine how much money one can receive: 1) The age of the (youngest) borrower. 2) The value of the home up to a limit (Maximum Claim amount - this is why zip code is important. Every county in the country has a FHA lending limit). And 3) the Expected Interest Rate.

It is important to note that there are two different interest rate numbers on every FHA/HECM reverse mortgage. We speak of "Initial Interest Rates" and "Expected Interest Rates." Think of the Initial Interest Rate as the Note Rate. This will be used to determine how much money will be eventually paid back. The Expected Interest Rate has one function – to help determine how much money one can get.

Without the following, you will not have enough information to use the National Reverse Mortgage Lenders Association's (NRMLA) reverse mortgage calculator. Therefore you will need the date of birth of each borrower; Value of the home: Zip Code; Outstanding mortgages and liens; However, only an individual that is trained to originate reverse mortgages, can provide you with exact figures, as they are familiar with all the reverse mortgage closing costs in their originating area. After you have the above information, go online to http://nrmla.edthosting.com. Please note that individuals specializing in originating reverse mortgages use proprietary originating software, not available to you. However, you will be able to get good ball park numbers.

In addition to this, our "Principal Limit" numbers noted in this article may not match the numbers you get, as the Expected Interest Rate is always changing. This rate is the yield on the 10 year bond plus a 1.5 margin for the monthly adjustable and a 3.1 margin for the annual adjustable. One will always receive more money from the monthly adjustable than they will from the annual adjustable. This is because the Expected Interest Rate is higher on the Annual loan. However, the interest rate cap on the annual is 5 points above the start rate and 10 points above the start rate on the monthly adjustable.

When the Expected Interest Rate goes up there is less money available. When it goes down there is more money available. Reverse mortgage originators receive these updates on a weekly basis. So the numbers can fluctuate from week to week. As I write this, the expected interest rate is 6.21%. Based on my 81 year old client's age, her $500,000 home, located in Nassau County, New York, will give her a Principal Limit of $266,650.65. The Principal Limit is really a starting point. It is from the Principal Limit that all things are deducted to get to the "Net available" to the borrower. Now if the Expected Interest Rate was 6.00% when the application was started, her Principal Limit would be $272,818.080. If when we started the application, the Expected Interest Rate was 6.35% then her starting Principal limit would be $263,748.33. Clearly you can see how the Expected Interest Rate affects the starting point. It is important to know that the Principal Limit is locked at time of application.

I noted above that the Principal Limit is nothing more than a starting point. Different costs and charges are then deducted. The resulting balance is what is left for our borrower. The first thing that is deducted is something called a Service Set Aside. In this client's case, her service set aside is $3882.05. Her Available Principal Limit is now $262,768.60. Next the closing costs get deducted. In the New York metropolitan area the total closing costs including origination fee, Mortgage insurance Premium and all typical closing costs on a home with a maximum claim amount of $362,790 will equal about $18,500.00. The equity in the home is paying for these costs. However some clients choose to pay the appraisal and termite inspection out of pocket. For a total out-of-pocket cost of $500, your client will have access to about a quarter of a million dollars to use any way that she wants.

Now it is important to talk about value. If the appraised value came in at $375,000 none of the numbers would change. If the value came in at $450,000 the numbers would not change. For reverse mortgage purposes, FHA caps how much of the home value it uses to determine how much money a senior borrower can get. What FHA is actually saying is this: It's nice that the value came in at $500,000 but for our purposes we will assume the value is not greater than $362,790 In the New York Metropolitan area, the FHA lending limit is $362,790. If the value of a home comes in below this limit, a borrower would get less money. If our borrower's home value came in at $275,000 her principal limit would be $202,125 instead of $266,650.65.

Now watch this. Let us say that you have a client that lives in a $500,000 home in upstate New York. Your client is the same age as mine, 81 years old. You would expect that your client would get the same amount of money as above discussed. Because your client lives in an area with a lending limit of $275,200 only this amount of the $500,000 home is counted toward determining how much money she can get. In this case your client's Principal Limit or starting point is $205,299.20. Because the Mortgage Insurance Premium, Origination Fee and Title Insurance Premiums are based upon a lower lending limit, the closing costs would be reduced to about $12,208.00

Just a few brief words about the other programs: The FNMA Home Keeper program is generally more conservative than FHA's program. When there are two borrowers, the amount received is reduced, as the lender has to wait longer to get repaid. This program is appropriate for single family homes, FNMA approved condos and HOAs.

If you have a borrower that lives in a high-value home, they may be able to realize more from the "jumbo" reverse mortgage program. Remember that age and value continue to be critical to determining how much money one can get. Let us say that you have a 62 year old client living in a $1,000,000 home. How much money can they get? If we assume that they live in the New York Metro area, where the FHA lending limit is $362,790, the Principal Limit based upon the current Expected Interest Rate as above noted is $194,092.65. The Principal Limit under the "jumbo program" currently is $168,800. (You cannot access the "jumbo" reverse mortgage program on the calculator. You must speak to a reverse mortgage originator. To find a reverse mortgage originator in your area, go to NRMLA's web site at www. reversemortgage.org and click on Lenders in your area.)

Now if this same individual was the same age as our client, 81 the numbers would be quite different. Because she is 81, her Principal Limit, under the "jumbo program," would then be $420,200. There are no lending limits under this program. This means that it does not matter where the property is located. The closing costs vary greatly depending upon which option your client picks. If they decide to take all the money in one shot, there are zero closing costs. Should they decide to take 75% of the funds upfront, then the closing costs are capped at $3500. Should they decide to draw the available funds on a monthly basis or take a partial draw or place the funds in the reverse mortgage line of credit, then the closing costs can exceed those costs for homes located in the highest FHA lending limit areas.

I have attempted to keep things simple. There is still so much more to talk about. You have the basics; I hope some of the mystery has been taken out of the process. No other loan program can currently fulfill the needs of those seniors that want to stay in their homes and live their hopes and dreams. It is important to become familiar with these programs as more and more lenders enter this market place. Many see this as just another program to keep business in the door as conventional mortgage business continues to decline. These companies do not care about your client nor do they possess the depth of knowledge that would permit them to intelligently explain this program to you and your clients.

Because people are living longer, a reverse mortgage can insure that your clients will not out live their money. The creation of this innovative program is significantly changing the lives of our elders.

It must Be thought About in Human terms (Not Numbers)

# Reverse Mortgages Should Be a Choice of First Resort (2003)

Seniors are becoming more savvy. They are asking more questions and demanding more answers about things that affect their lives. Nothing has the power to change their lives forever like a reverse mortgage can. Much has been written about reverse mortgages. More has been transmitted by word of mouth. Everyone it seems has an opinion or a comment about them. The problem is that much of this information is wrong. One basic fact remains. If you do or think the same thing each and every day, you will not get a different result. The result will always be the same. If, on the other hand, you change your thought pattern and take different action, you have the ability to make your life immeasurably better. This is what a reverse mortgage can do. It can make your life immeasurably better. Keep reading.

The basic question that every senior should ask themselves: Why don't I have a reverse mortgage now?

If the answer is that I can't qualify for a mortgage, your thinking is off base. There is no income, asset or credit qualification. *only true No doc*

If the answer is that I have to make monthly mortgage payments, your thinking is off base. A borrower never makes mortgage payments with a reverse mortgage.

If the answer is that the bank will own my home, your thinking is off base. The borrower continues to own the home when a reverse mortgage is placed against the home.

If the answer is that the out-of-pocket expenses are too high, then your thinking is off-base. Usually there are no upfront fees. All other closing costs can be rolled into the loan amount.

If the answer is that my heirs are personally responsible for paying back the loan, your thinking is off base. Even if the value of the home plummets, so that the amount due on the reverse mortgage is greater than the value of the home, the most the bank can get for repayment is the value of the home. Your heirs will never have to pay one penny.

If the answer is that the closing costs in general are too high, your thinking is off-base. It is not only about the numbers; it must be thought about in human terms. For example, you must ask, "What is it worth to me?" I bet you didn't know that a significant amount of the closing costs gets paid directly to the government. This mortgage insurance provides comfort to seniors who are relying on a bank to continue to make payments to the borrower under the reverse mortgage program. Banks have been known to fail.

With a reverse mortgage, as long as you use the home as a primary residence, keep the home in good repair, pay the property taxes, and pay the homeowners insurance, you can live in the home as long as you like without having to repay the loan.

While seniors would love to leave their homes to their children mortgage-free, many cannot. Seniors are out-living their money. The point is that most children do not want their parents to live a life of hardship. With a reverse mortgage, generally there is plenty of equity left over.

The parents get the benefit today, the children get the benefit tomorrow: Perfect. The parents win and the children win.

# Consequences (2004)

Make a decision today. Consequences will flow from that decision. Refuse to make a decision today consequences will still flow from that non decision. Even when you delay making a decision, consequences will continue to flow.

Whether you take action or remain inactive you will feel the affects from your choices. Senior citizens and their family particularly, often ignore the consequences of their actions (or non actions.) Often they are not prepared to face the stark choices staring them in the face.

Seniors today and their baby boomer children together are not stepping up to the plate to confront the choices that the universe is begging them to confront.

The legal and financial planning communities place a premium on planning for a client's retirement. Yet they do not adequately protect the client's stake in their future. Seniors and their families are refusing to look at the consequences of not dying. Living a long life is a near certainty. Planning for it is a necessity. Years ago people got cancer, a heart attack or a stroke and died. A death sentence was the norm. Today people get old, they get sick they live, they need long term care and they need money. That is the new reality. Not dying will have a tremendous impact on the family.

Your children do not want to take care of you. If there are not adequate choices they will make an effort to take care of you but they do not WANT to take care of you. Many have jobs, family & other responsibilities. The burden of care giving can rip a family apart. More children will spend more time taking care of their parents than their parents took care of you. Many children will suffer the loss of their jobs and the loss of promotions because there is no money to provide otherwise.

When principal is invaded a financial death spiral ensues. So the question that attorneys must ask their clients; the question that accountants must ask their clients; the question that financial planners must ask their older clients is this:

HAVE YOU CONSIDERED THE CONSEQUENCES NOT DYING WILL HAVE ON YOU AND YOUR FAMILY? Only by asking this question can you open the door of conversation to talk about finances, estate planning, Medicaid planning, gifting, methods of preserving the parents' estate, end of life and funeral planning. This one question is a powerful question that can lead to solutions that protect the family unit.

# A Reverse Mortgage Is Just The Medicine
## An Aging America Needs (2004)

There was a time, when America was young. At the signing of the Constitution the median age was 16. Life expectancy was a mere thirty five. In a short historical span of over 230 years, much has changed. Our country's population is growing old. This trend will continue at an increasing speed.

Consider this: In 1900 one in twenty people were at least 65. Today one in eight have reached this milestone. In July of 1983, a startling thing occurred. For the first time in the history of the country the number of people 65 and over was greater than the number of teenagers. By the year 2050 there will be twice as many people in this category than teenagers.

Consider this: According to the last census there were 35 million people in this country that have reached their 65th birthday. This number will double by the year 2050. Today this country has more people 65 or over than the entire population of Canada.

Consider this: In the "good old days" one grew old, got sick then died. Today, one grows old, gets sick and continues to live. 85% of our seniors have one chronic condition. 30% have three or more chronic conditions. The explosion in the senior market place today is in the 85 and over age bracket. It is estimated that by 2050 this age group will be 20 million strong.

Seniors own about 23% of the housing units in this country. Of the 16 million homes owned by our seniors 12 million are owned mortgage free. Clearly they do not wish to make those monthly mortgage payments. This is the conundrum. Seniors are among the poorest and wealthiest groups of people in this country. Until recently prying that equity loose usually required the sale of the home or required that they qualify for a conventional loan. Today there is a third way. A reverse mortgage could very well be the medicine that cures those financial maladies.

A reverse mortgage is a special kind of loan. It is special because the senior who is at least 62 years of age never has to make monthly mortgage payments. It is special because all reverse mortgage loans are non-recourse loans. This means that there is no personal liability. If the amount that is owed is greater than the value of the house (assume that the home depreciated in value during the term of the reverse mortgage), then the most the bank can receive is the value of the home. This is an incredible feature. Compare this to the loan that you have on your home now. If the same scenario happened, your bank would sue you personally for the difference. This could never happen with a reverse mortgage.

It is special because it frees up a portion of the equity that a senior can covert into cash. It provides a senior with a wonderful way to reach this equity without selling and without obtaining a loan that they have to make monthly payments on. Many surveys indicate that a majority of seniors prefer to remain in their homes.

It is special because the senior can receive the proceeds in a variety of ways: They can receive money each month, take a lump sum, a partial lump sum or put the money in a reverse mortgage line of credit. Once they make a choice, they can always change their minds. They are never locked into a particular way to receive their money.

It is a special loan because it becomes a lifesaver for both the children and the parents. Over $2 billion a month is spent in this country by children who are financially helping their parents. Many cannot do it anymore. The adult children have to put money away for their own retirement and for the college education of their own children. The parents, on the other hand, have reclaimed their independence and their dignity. In essence, the reverse mortgage transfigures the strained relationship into a loving relationship free from "required" financial obligations.

Because of this features, it offers to our financially ailing seniors a cure for their ills. It offers hope that they can realize their fondest dreams. A reverse mortgage could be just the right medicine that protects the senior from the financial germs of life.

make that special phone call - don't delay
any Longer. Let's Bring a Better quality
of live + less Financial stress to those
we love.

# The Changing Face of Reverse Mortgages (2007)

Although the reverse mortgage concept has been around since the early 60's, its terms, provisions and conditions were desultory at best. Underwriting standardization occurred after Congress authorized HUD to create the FHA/HECM program in 1987. About 92% of all reverse mortgage programs obtained are of the FHA/HECM variety. Therefore most of our attention will be focused on this program. (The other kind of program is the non government insured variety. These programs are often referred to as "proprietary" or "private brand.")

Reverse mortgages are the hottest topic in the mortgage industry today. It is easy to see why. It is estimated that 4.3 trillion dollars in home equity is currently available; this will more than double in 10 years. Eighty-nine percent of all reverse mortgages closed since 1990 have been originated since 2000. The yearly growth in production since 2000 has grown by a factor of 10. However, the over all market penetration is hovering at about 1 percent. Clearly clients are demanding that their attorney, accountant, financial advisor, et al. become knowledgeable about this solution. (Moreover, these advisors must be able to explain the reverse mortgage concept and answer its complicated questions.)

Next year the oldest baby boomers will start turning 62. Because of the impending growth in this market place, Wall Street has taken a lead role in changing the industry. Over the past six months, the industry has witnessed an impressive amount of substantive modifications. Additionally, HUD, NRMLA & AARP have been instrumental in making other innovative refinements to the program. This article will highlight a few of the salient program changes that have transmuted a rather prosaic program into a dynamic and vibrant program that will continue to change the lives of seniors across the country. This article will set forth important future changes that should occur when certain bills pass Congress.

The first decisive change to the program occurred in 2000 with the elimination of the equity sharing option. This option allowed the lender to receive a portion of the appreciation on the subject property during the time the reverse mortgage was in place. This was in addition to the accrued interest. The industry learned a very expensive lesson. This egregious practice significantly retarded the growth of the program. Sadly, many people still erroneously believe that this practice exists today.

The next decisive change occurred in September 2003. Up until that time, a senior borrower would not know how much money would be available, until closing. This created a great deal of uncertainty and angst, as the borrower never knew what to expect! Today, the borrower knows that

71

they can not receive less that the amount disclosed at application. (This presupposes that the assumed property value is an accurate reflection of the appraised value).

In essence, the rate that helps determine how much your client can receive is now locked in. However, should this rate change in your clients' favor, the possibility exists that they could receive more than that amount disclosed at application. This rate lock protection was further changed in August, 2006 by increasing the duration of the rate lock to 120 days from the time the case number is obtained.

From the inception of the program, through 2006, all reverse mortgage loans were adjustable. The monthly adjustable was the preferred choice over the yearly adjustable (particularly when the margin on the annual adjustable climbed to 3.1%).

The margin used to calculate the monthly adjustable note rate and the attendant expected interest rate had not changed in 18 years. The margin was 1.50%. However, 2007 ushered in a monthly adjustable rate utilizing a lower margin (by at least 50 basis points). This resulted in providing significantly more money to a senior borrower. 2007 also saw the introduction of the fixed rate FHA/HECM reverse mortgage and the proprietary fixed rate reverse mortgage. (At the time this article was submitted, severe disruptions in the mortgage market were occurring. It remains to be seen whether these secondary market concerns will have a spillover effect upon reverse mortgage pricing).

Closing costs are a concern to some. A few proprietary programs have zero closing costs when a borrower takes the entire proceeds in one lump sum. Besides this, there are moves on several fronts to lower the closing costs on the FHA/HECM loans. The FHA Modernization Bill and the Expanding Homeownership Act of 2007 seek to make seminal revisions to the FHA/HECM reverse mortgage: lower both the origination fees and the upfront FHA mortgage insurance premium; permit the FHA reverse mortgage program to include co-op apartments; allow purchase transactions; increase the amount of the home value used in calculating benefit amounts and create a single national loan limit. These create exciting possibilities.

HUD has also agreed to permit the use of different indices in determining interest rates. While this was a concession to the secondary markets that are more comfortable using the LIBOR index (London Interbank Offered Rate), it should also have the salutary effect of lowering rates. This in turn will put more money into the pockets of your clients.

Because reverse mortgages are the hottest topic in the mortgage industry, many mortgage companies are jumping on the proverbial band wagon. It is hard to believe that just a few years ago, it was not an easy task to locate a mortgage company that was originating reverse mortgages. Today, the program is becoming ubiquitous. Therefore you must become the sentinel for your clients as novice reverse mortgage companies flood the market place. Many of these companies think the senior market is a market that can be conquered with slick advertising and a hard-sell philosophy. Today, everyone in this field is calling themselves a "reverse mortgage expert." This term is quickly becoming a bromide and will soon have little meaning.

While eighty six percent of those 62 or over are aware that the program exists, half are uncertain how the program works. Twenty five percent of the respondents according to a recent Harris poll had a very favorable opinion of the program. Thirty nine percent had no opinion. Thirty six percent had an unfavorable opinion of the product. This shows that there is still a lot of education to be done.

Attorneys must be part of this education. Reverse mortgage knowledge will be another arrow in your planning quiver. Attorneys will be the front line of defense to insure that their clients have a favorable outcome. You will need to protect your clients from inexperienced companies that provide little guidance and poor advice.

# The Top Ten Reasons Why Your Clients Should Consider A Reverse Mortgage (2005)

Listed and explained below are the ten top reasons why your clients need to consider obtaining a reverse mortgage. I underline the word consider. For purposes of this article, it is assumed that the home is a primary residence and your client(s) are at least 62 years of age. This means that if two people own the home each must be 62. While there are other considerations, only my top ten are explained below.

### Reason # 10
The FHA/ HECM programs contain much flexibility. They can access the proceeds in a variety of ways. The manner in which these proceeds can be obtained can be changed from time to time. The program can also work with a life estate and a trust. After a significant period of time has gone by, and assuming an increase in value of the home and an increase in the maximum claim amount, a reverse mortgage can be refinanced with another reverse mortgage.

### Reason # 9
The numbers tell a compelling story. Your clients can reclaim their lives and again live with independence and dignity.

a. People are outliving their money. Today, in this country there are more than 35 million people that are 65 and over.

b. More people than ever have reached age 100. The last three census reports illustrate the number of people reaching age 100(rounded off): 1980 15,000   1990 28,000 2000   52,000

c. 85% of seniors 65% and older have at least one chronic condition.

d. Children helping mom and/or dad are spending in excess of $2 billion per month for their parents' groceries, support and medical needs.

e. Many 401Ks feel like "101Ks"

### Reason # 8
Contrary to what many people believe, a reverse mortgage is quite affordable. Depending upon the type of reverse mortgage chosen, the out of pocket closing costs usually range from $0 to $575. The balance of the closing costs comes right out of the equity of the house. It will never come out of the pocket of your senior clients.

### Reason # 7
Imagine for a moment, that your clients obtained a conventional loan from their bank. History teaches us that many seniors that go to their banks to borrow do so in the following manner: LET'S SAY THAT YOUR CLIENT

RECEIVED A LOAN IN THE AMOUNT OF $100,000. $80,000 IS SPENT. The balance is put aside so that those monthly mortgage payments can be made. When that money is gone they can no longer make those mortgage payments. A foreclosure or sale becomes a real possibility. This is exactly what they sought to avoid when they obtained that original loan. Now suppose that your client used the same amount of money from an entity that provides reverse mortgages. They would never be required to make those monthly mortgage payments. The loan becomes due only when the home is no longer a primary residence, upon the death of the survivor or the home is sold.. The point is that the home is sold only when your clients no longer have a use for it.

**Reason # 6**
Imagine that your clients worked so hard for much of their lives to pay off that initial mortgage….now it is time their home paid them back. What an incredible thought…giving your clients the peace of mind that they desire.

**Reason # 5**
When your clients obtain a reverse mortgage they will be easing the tremendous monetary burden their adult children are experiencing. Adult children that help their parents cannot do that AND take care of their own family's financial affairs. They cannot put money away for their own retirement nor for their children's college education.

Some adult children are even forced to quit their job or decline a promotion, when they are compelled to become the caregiver. This can place a strain on the family unit. When a reverse mortgage is obtained, the parents have reclaimed their independence and dignity. The adult children can finally focus financially upon their family needs. A reverse mortgage becomes a lifesaver for both families.

**Reason # 4**
Qualifying for a reverse mortgage is rather EASY. There is no income, asset or credit requirements. They must "own" the home, be 62 and it must be a primary residence. That is it. Then it will be determined whether it is suitable.

**Reason # 3**
A reverse mortgage usually contains a growth factor in the line of credit option. Let us compare this to taking out a credit line with a bank. Assume that your clients take out a $100,000 credit line with a bank. They haven't drawn down any of the money. After 5 years you would still have $100,000 at your disposal. When you take out a reverse mortgage, and you choose the credit line option, you could have a lot more in the account at the end of

5 years. (The amount in the line of credit contains a built in growth factor that increases at the current interest note rate plus 50 basis points-tax free [FHA/HECM]). In actuality, the credit limit is merely increasing. When the loan becomes due, only the amount taken out of the line of credit will be paid back, with the appropriate interest and fees. The amount that has not been accessed can not be used when the loan becomes due.

## Reason # 2
When your clients get a reverse mortgage they can accomplish many financial goals. Actually they are limited by their creativity. Let me list some of the goals clients have accomplished:

> Pay off credit cards
> Pay off a current mortgage
> Pay off tax liens
> Stop a foreclosure action
> Purchase a long term care policy
> Hire a caregiver or provide home care
> Purchase an annuity
> Make repairs to the home
> Travel
> Build that second/vacation home
> Provide gifts to your children and/or grandchildren in need
> Purchase life insurance.

With a "jumbo" reverse mortgage they can do even more.

## Reason # 1 WHY YOUR CLIENTS MUST CONSIDER A REVERSE MORTGAGE
Simply put: IT WILL CHANGE THEIR LIVES FOREVER!!!!!!!!!!!
Never again will they have to figure out or worry about how their bills will be paid. Never again will they have to choose between medications. Never again will they have to make choices between how much less they have to be satisfied with. Your clients will dare to dream again of a better time. They can grab that piece of "financial immunity." They can create their "New Deal." In 1933 President Roosevelt created the New Deal. He put money into the pockets of all Americans. Now your clients can create their own personal New Deal and put money into their pockets. Only they have the power.

# Twenty-Five Positive Lessons
# I Learned From My Elder Clients (2006)

In the East, Elders are revered for their wisdom and insight. In the West, the antithesis is true. For the past 5 years I have been working with our elders. Along the way, they have inspired me and energized me. Many have experienced the adversity that comes during war time and tough economic conditions. For the most part, many have maintained a wonderful positive attitude that I feel compelled to share with you. Others have remained bitter and upset that their lives have not turned out better. Interestingly, the latter group sees themselves as victims, whereas the former view themselves as having control over their future. I would like to share with you the twenty five positive lessons my clients have taught me.

1. My goal in life is to give birth to my true self.
2. Each day I remember to plant a little seed. Each kindness I give, like the seed, will eventually blossom into a wonderful thing.
3. I have found that living in the past takes away from my future.
4. My positive attitude forces me to believe that no matter what happens-good can flourish.
5. It is the tiny steps that really make the true difference in life.
6. Always shoot for the moon. That way you can't miss. At worst, you will land among the stars.
7. I am the architect of my life. It is my choice to build it or destroy it.
8. I don't have a college degree, but I have a great education because I constantly read.
9. Over the years, I have made plenty of mistakes. Mistakes are the real teacher of life.
10. Every choice I make is like a fork in the road. The choice takes me in a different direction and leads me to a new adventure.
11. I am not growing old. I am growing wiser.
12. It is never too late to do things you were told you could never do.
13. You can't learn something new if you can't experience it.
14. My past and future are still in front of me.
15. Better than a pill is the reduction of stress.
16. Choose your words carefully. They can be dangerous like a weapon, or beautiful like a musical instrument.
17. I never live in the past because there is always tomorrow.
18. The only thing that matters more than family is family.
19. It is easy to have a positive attitude because I toss the "negative garbage"

in the trash can at the end of each day.

20. "Yes" opens up many doors. "No" closes them.

21. Tomorrow gives me an opportunity to get better.

22. The more wrinkles I get, the wiser I become.

23. Even though my gas tank is "empty," I am raring to go.

24. Asking "Why me?" makes me a victim. Asking "What else?" makes me a winner.

25. Learning is the exercise that keeps my mind strong.

# CONGRESSIONAL TESTIMONY
## Submitted to the U.S. House of Representatives
## on November 15, 2005

Thank you Chairman Ney, Ranking member Waters, and members of the Committee for the opportunity to appear before the Committee to address it on the issue of Reverse Mortgages. I am an attorney and have been originating and writing about reverse mortgages for the past four years. I am Executive Vice President of Senior Funding Group in Hicksville, NY and originate reverse mortgages throughout the New York Metro area.

Quite simply reverse mortgages are changing the lives of seniors across the country. This is the second time that seniors and or the parents of seniors have become financial pioneers: This time with reverse mortgages. Many years ago, our seniors of today pioneered the concept of the thirty year loan. Many of the arguments that were used to dissuade seniors from obtaining a thirty-year loan when the program was first introduced in 1935 are the same arguments being used today by those who do not think a reverse mortgage is a sound idea. The thirty-year loan marked a significant change how seniors and or their parents purchased and/or refinanced their homes. (Prior to the creation of the thirty year loan, loans were five year interest only balloon notes.) Individuals were signing newly created documents some considered dangerous but today these documents are considered standard. People were warned that they would lose their homes and go broke if they signed their names to these documents. People were even told that it is impossible to make payments for such a long period of time. The home will be lost to foreclosure. However, history has shown that it was the thirty-year loan that helped to create the initial housing boom and it was the thirty-year loan that allowed people to own their homes. And it can be said that it is the reverse mortgage that is keeping seniors safely in their homes.

The bottom line question is this: What other program allows seniors, who have already made the decision to stay in their home, to convert some of the equity into cash, without making monthly mortgage payments and without the vetting of their income, assets or credit? Currently there is no other program. I have prepared a rather extensive 12 page report on the reverse mortgage program. I wish to request the Chairman's permission to include as part of my testimony, this 12 page report. Today, in the few minutes that I have I would like to explore with you key important facts that need to be put into focus.

Clearly this country's population is getting older. Seniors as a group are facing financial turmoil. Some have lost money in the stock market: Others have witnessed their pension plan evaporate before their eyes; Others never expected to live so long: Yet others simply neglected to do even the most basic financial planning.

At a time when property taxes are soaring out of control, prescription drugs are more costly, home heating oil is higher than in recent years, as is gasoline prices, many of our clients are looking toward their homes to help them reclaim their lives.

A reverse mortgage is a different and special kind of loan that is easy to get if one is at least 62 years of age and they own their own home. This kind of loan is different and special because as I said there is no income, asset or credit requirements and there are no monthly mortgage payments to be made to a lender. The third reason it is a special loan is because there is no personal liability, as these loans are non recourse. The borrower can get the proceeds from the loan in a variety of ways. To wit: Monthly payments (term or tenure), lump sum, partial lump sum, line of credit or in combination.

The essence of what a reverse mortgage is can be described with the following picture. I say to my clients, "Imagine that you are shaking hands with their home and saying Look I've taken care of you for so many years" and the home is replying, "That's right, now it is my turn to take care of you."

I have my clients focus on this picture because the loan itself is a bit complex. That picture helps to keep it simple. The reality is that three things determine how much money one receives. The age of the youngest borrower, the value of the home up to a certain limit( maximum claim amount- the lesser of the appraised value or FHA lending limit for the area )and the yield on the ten year bond." Explaining what the expected interest rate is and how the yield effects the principal limit is a challenge in and of itself. Then one needs to go on to explain what the principal limit is and what the service set aside is.

The loan program itself needs to be made simpler. I applaud HUD, NRMLA and AARP in their continuous effort to make the program better. Adding hundreds of new counselors will make the process go faster. The amount of new counselors will increase the overall counseling capacity to over 90,000 cases per year; The newly created principal limit disclosure takes away the uncertainty caused by a fluctuating bond market. But there is still more to accomplish:

Consult- First - Or After loan gets started

The volume of documents must be reduced. The time to get a loan to closing must also be reduced.

Having one national lending limit for reverse mortgages will obviate the inequity that now exists. For example, take an individual living in the New York metropolitan area, where the FHA lending limit is the highest ($312,895). The client is 75 and lives in a home valued at $320,000. Based on current rates, the Principal limit would be $212,455.71. Take a different individual with the same age who also lives in a home valued at $320,000 . The only difference is the FHA lending limit. An individual living in Port St Lucie County, Florida where the FHA limit is only $237,000, will have a current principal limit of only $160,923.

Reducing the upfront mortgage insurance premium is also an important priority. The top MIP amount is currently $6257.90 This money should be placed in the pockets of our seniors. It is also important to eliminate the service set aside fee. While technically not a closing cost, this fee reduces the amount that a senior can realize. This fee can range from about $1500 to over $5000.

HUD has been reviewing for some time, whether to allow their program to embrace co-ops. Currently there is one national proprietary program that will permit a reverse mortgage on a co-op apartment. However, it only applies to co-op apartments in the State of New York. There is however, some hope that this proprietary program will be expanded into additional states. The processing time on this proprietary program takes 3 to 6 months. The HECM reverse mortgage is currently excluding a significant segment of seniors that live in certain big cities where co-op apartments are prevalent. In essence, we are saying to a defined group of seniors that you can not get a reverse mortgage even though you meet the age requirement.

The growth in recent years has been staggering. Yet in my opinion the reverse mortgage program should be bigger than it is. Many professionals do not understand the program and many seniors talk about the common misconceptions as if they were absolutely true.

For Example:
Many seniors believe that the bank will own the home if they obtain a reverse mortgage. This is not true. The basic requirement is that the senior applicant must own the home.

Many seniors believe that the loan becomes due upon the death of the first to die. This is not true. It becomes due on the death of the survivor.

Many seniors believe that monthly mortgage payments still need to be made. This is not true. There are no monthly mortgage payments.

Many seniors believe that the closing costs must come directly out of their pocket. This is not true. All the closing costs can be financed with the reverse mortgage loan.

Many seniors believe that the reverse mortgage proceeds will adversely affect their Social Security payment. This is not true. The proceed are not considered income. It is a loan.

Many seniors believe that a reverse mortgage is not necessary if they do Medicaid planning. This is not true. Reverse mortgages offer a way a way to assist Medicaid planning by taking money out of the house today, while starting the running of the look back period.

Many seniors believe that a reverse mortgage requirement is that the applicant must be in good health. This is not true. Many clients get the reverse mortgage so they have adequate funds to pay for custodial care in the home.

Many seniors believe that reverse mortgages are only for the poor. This is not true. Seniors in every income bracket have obtained a reverse mortgage.

Many seniors believe that their heirs will become personally responsible for paying back the loan. This is not true. The loan is non recourse.

At the same time many seniors do not understand how they can harness the incredible power of a reverse mortgage. It must be noted that the principal limit and the line of credit contain a growth factor that provides much more money over the life of the loan than the amount noted in the principal limit. You will never find this feature in any other kind of loan product. For example, if one obtained a home equity line of credit from their neighborhood bank for $100,000 that they did not access for 2 years how much would their line of credit be worth after this 2 year period? The answer is the same $100,000. Their line of credit would not grow. However, a reverse mortgage line of credit would be worth much more than $100,000 under this scenario. Under the FHA program, the line of credit will grow at 50 basis points above the note rate. The current note rate is 5.85%.

Many parents believe that the home is the only financial vehicle that will protect them from their current financial storm. Leaving the home mortgage free to their kids is not the focal point. While seniors know that money is not the most important thing, they also know that the lack of money affects everything that is important. A reverse mortgage in essence becomes a lifesaver for the parent and their adult children as well. Children in this country are giving over 2 billion dollars each moth to help their parents. They can not do it anymore. They need to put money away for their own retirement and for their kids' college education. They can not do this and continue to give to mom and or dad. When the parent gets the reverse mortgage, it reconfigures the family relationship. The parent can reclaim their financial independence and dignity. The children can focus upon their family.

And finally let me  say that while we have come a long way since the inception of what I call  the modern day reverse mortgage (which was authorized by Congress in 1987), working together, we can continue to find ways to make the program better. Today seniors are sitting on two trillion dollars of home assets which represent about 950 million dollars in reverse mortgage funds.  A confluence of forces have come together to place reverse mortgages directly in the limelight. The National Governors Association, the Centers for Medicare and Medicaid Services and the National Council On Aging view reverse mortgages as an important financial and economic tool that is both helpful to our senior community and helpful to the local, state and federal government as well. Rebalancing this country's long term care and medical delivery systems together with addressing the fear of impoverishment will continue to be important considerations.

Accordingly the program needs to remain strong and sustaining. Eliminating an artificial cap that seems to get in the way every few years is important. Sending a message to the reverse mortgage community and more importantly to seniors that this program is here to stay sends a very important message. Finding alternative housing sources is also an important message. Seniors and their advocates need to create alternative housing choices. As 76 million baby boomers age, having choices and flexibility will become very critical as well.

# Glossary

## Dennis Haber's Glossary
## Of Key Terms You Need to Understand

\* *Applies to FHA/HECM*
\*\* *Applies to Proprietary Program*

**Principal Limit \* \*\***
The gross amount one can borrow based upon the age of the youngest borrower (if there are two or more borrowers), value of the home (up to the FHA lending limit in your county) and the Expected Interest Rate. Think of these three things as "ingredients" or "component parts." The amount represented by the Principal Limit I also call the "Starting Point" or "Benefit Amount." It is from this amount that items get deducted to arrive at the net amount you can use for yourself after considering closing costs, the service set aside and liens, if any, that need to be paid.

**Expected Interest Rate \***
The Expected Interest Rate has only one function: To help determine how much money you can get. To put it another way, the Expected Interest Rate helps determine your available loan advances. Accordingly, under the FHA program, it is a constant interest rate that is used to calculate these loan advances. If you think of a see-saw you will understand how the expected interest rate affects the Principal Limit. Picture you and a friend on a see-saw. When you go up, your friend goes down. So when the Expected Interest Rate goes up, the Principal Limit would go down. When the Expected Interest Rate goes down, the Principal Limit goes up. This caused a lot of fear in the earlier years, because a reverse mortgage borrower would never know just how much money they would receive because of this "see-saw effect."

Now the Principal Limit is protected. When the closing occurs within the prescribed period of time, a borrower is protected from getting fewer funds, even if at the time of closing the Expected Interest Rate is higher. On the other hand, the borrower will have access to more funds if the Expected Interest Rate is lower than it was at the time the application was taken.

**FHA Lending Limit \***
A limit is placed on how much of your home's value will be used to determine the above noted Principal Limit. This amount usually changes each year. Every county in the country has such a limit. This amount can differ greatly from county to county. You will maximize what you can get from a value perspective if the value of your home equals or exceeds the lending limit in your area. A value greater than the lending limit will not increase your Principal Limit. On the other hand a lesser value will decrease how much money one can get (Principal Limit). So when considering a reverse mortgage, you may wish to find out what the FHA lending limit is in your area. Future legislation may allow the HECM program to use a single national limit or smilar structure.

**Service Set Aside \***
In reality, the Service Set Aside is a calculated amount based on age and life expectancy that is deducted from the Principal Limit. No amount is actually set aside. It merely represents an additional small amount of equity that will not be converted into reverse mortgage proceeds.

**Initial Interest Rate \* \*\***
I call it the "note rate." Every loan contains an interest rate. The interest rate can either be fixed or adjustable. As the industry further matures, different indices and margins (adjustable rate) will be used. This rate ultimately determines how much interest will accrue over the life of the loan.

**TALC (Total Annual Loan Cost) \* \*\***
This is the average interest rate that would produce the amount owed based on a particular choice of receiving the money limited by the non recourse feature found in reverse mortgage loans. This also includes the costs to obtain the loan.

TALC rates are usually higher in the early years because the closing costs will represent a greater percentage of the outstanding balance. As time passes and more money is accessed, the closing costs will represent a smaller portion of this outstanding balance. Therefore, these rates will be lower in later years as the balance continues to increase.

A higher TALC rate usually means that there is more equity in the home. A lower TALC rate usually means that the borrower is taking a greater amount out in the early years. This means that there will be less equity in the home, when the loan finally gets paid off.

TALC rates take into account the term of the loan; the payment plan and appreciation factors and are merely projections.

**Tenure Payment ***
A monthly payment option that will never stop as long as the borrower is in the home, using it as a primary residence. Think of this type of monthly payment as a bucket of money that will always be full.

**Modified Tenure Payment ***
A monthly payment option that is also combined with the line of credit.

**Term Payment * ****
A monthly payment option that will stop after a period of time has expired. The amount selected to be received is in an amount greater than the tenure payment option. Think of this as a bucket of money that will become empty after a certain period of time has passed.

**Modified Term Payment * ****
A monthly payment option that will stop after a period of time has expired, combined with a line of credit option.

**Line of Credit * ****
A reverse mortgage line of credit (LOC) option is significantly different than a typical line of credit. Let's say that you have a $200,000 LOC from your neighborhood bank. You have not used the line for two years. How much would you have in the Line of Credit? $200,000.

How much money would you have in the line after two years, with a reverse mortgage LOC? The answer is an amount greater than the $200,000. The line contains a growth factor that increases the amount one can borrow. (Actually the credit limit is increasing.) This growth factor has no income tax implication. It simply increases the amount one can borrow on their reverse mortgage loan. Many reverse mortgage programs provide a growth factor in their line of credit. Some do not.

**HECM Loan** *
Whether referring to a Home Equity Conversion Mortgage (HECM), HUD, or FHA, one is referring to the same type of government insured loan.

**Maximum Claim Amount** *
This is the lesser of the FHA limit in your area or the appraised value of your home.

**Basic Loan Maturity Events** * **
The loan becomes due upon death of the surviving borrower; sale of home; or the home is no longer the primary residence of any borrower.

**Mortgage Insurance** *
Protects the lender against the consequences of the outstanding reverse mortgage balance being greater than the value of the home after the maturity event occurs. In other words, it protects the lender (up to a point) from the risk of not realizing payment in full.

**Proprietary Loan** **
A proprietary loan refers to a non-government insured loan. These loans are partially modeled after the HECM; yet these loans contain the basic reverse mortgage features which distinguish a reverse mortgage from a conventional mortgage. It usually has limitations on the ways you can access the funds. The Fannie Mae Home Keeper program is one such example.

**Non Recourse Loan** * **
Reverse mortgage loans do not permit a borrower to be personally liable. A lender cannot look toward any other assets of the borrower. The lender can only look to the value of the home for repayment.

**Equity Protection** **
Some programs contain an Equity Protection feature. It insures at the time of application that a predetermined amount of equity is guaranteed to be available to your heirs. In the event that amount actually due to the lender is greater than the protected predetermined amount, the lender will reduce the amount that is due.

## FOR PROFESSIONALS

HUD Handbook 4235.1 Revision No 1  (www.hudclips.org)
HUD Handbook 4060.1, Revision No.2
HUD Mortgagee Letters  (www.hud.gov/offices/hsg/mltrmenu.cfm)
Code of Federal Regulations  (http://ecfr.gpoaccess.gov)
Title 24: Housing & Urban Development
Part 206: Home Equity Conversion Mortgage Insurance

## FOR CONSUMERS

*Reverse Mortgages For Dummies®*
by Sarah Glendon Lyons & John E. Lucas (Wiley Publishing 2005)

*The New Reverse Mortgage Formula: How to Convert Home Equity Into Tax Free Income*
by Tom Kelley (John Wiley & Sons, Inc. 2005)

*Retire On Your House Using Real Estate To Secure Your Retirement*
by Gillette Edmunds & James Keene (John Wiley & Sons  2006)

*The 7 Powers of Questions*
by Dorothy Leeds (Berkley Publishing Group 2000)

*How Not To Go Broke at 102*
by Adriane Berg (John Wiley & Sons 2004)

AARP (www.aarp.org)

National Academy of Elder Law Attorneys (www.NAELA.org):
National membership directory

National Center For Home Equity Conversion (www.reverse.org)

*Just the FAQS: Answers to Common Questions About Reverse Mortgages*
from the National Reverse Mortgage Lenders Association (www.reversemortgage.org)

*Use Your Home To Stay At Home* from National Council On Aging (www.ncoa.org)

*Happily Ever After....Expert Advice for Achieving the Retirement of Your Dreams*
14 professional advisors provide valuable insight on topics of importance to retirees
Compiled & edited by Lyn Fisher & Sydney LeBlanc (Financial Forum, Inc 2007)

## OTHER ARTICLES BY DENNIS HABER

*Reverse Mortgages: Confusion reigns in New York*
*Reverse Mortgages to the rescue*
*What my clients are doing with their reverse mortgages*

# Index

# 3 ways to
# BRING DENNIS TO YOUR FIRM!

**1. Brand your organization with your own Book Cover:**
Your elderly clients and their families will appreciate the simple-to-understand format of Dennis Haber's book, "Piggy Bank Your Home." Ask us how we can print a custom cover with your organization's name!

**2. Train your professional associates on Reverse Mortgages:**
Do your colleages know the details that are so easily explained in "Piggy Bank Your Home"? Dennis Haber is a sought-after expert on reverse mortgages. Through interactive exercises, Dennis will ensure your associates explain reverse mortgages the right way, to help elderly clients and their families.

**3. Invite Dennis Haber to give a keynote address:**
Your next conference should be fun and educational: Dennis Haber's style is a brilliant mix of both. Through humor and case anecdotes, Dennis will help your organization appreciate how to properly address the growing trend of reverse mortgages.

## Ask Dennis your questions... 516.822.1020
## info@dennishaber.com

94

## About The Author

Dennis Haber is a distinguished member of the New York State Bar Association. In 2005, he submitted testimony to Congress on H.R. 2892 *Reverse Mortgages to Help America's Seniors Act* and H.R. 3859 *To Establish the Inter Agency Council on Meeting the Housing & Service Needs of Seniors.* Dennis is frequently interviewed by the media for his expertise on reverse mortgages.

Dennis also helped reduce title charges on reverse mortgages by explaining reverse mortgage concepts to the Title Insurance Rate Service Association (TIRSA), the rate service organization and statistical agent licensed by the Superintendent of the state of New York.

Dennis has also been published in regional and national publications including Elder Law Attorney, New York Law Journal, Real Estate Weekly, Senior Market Advisor, EA Journal, Nassau Lawyer and Suffolk Lawyer, to name a few. He has also been a featured "Ask the Expert" columnist in Newsday, and been featured in Long Island Business News. He has written an accredited course on reverse mortgages for the Wealth Preservation Institute.

He has presented reverse mortgage seminars to mortgage industry trade groups, bar associations, accountant & financial planning organizations. He also acts as a consultant to many professionals throughout the country who wish to give their clients complete and accurate information on reverse mortgages.

In 2006, the National Reverse Mortgage Lenders Association recognized Dennis' outstanding achievements by presenting him with an award for exemplary service to the industry. Dennis has served on the advisory council to the largest reverse mortgage lender in the USA.

In addition to authoring *Piggy Bank Your Home*, Dennis Haber has contributed to *Happily Ever After....Expert Advice for Achieving the Retirement of Your Dreams.* He is currently working on two additional books that will be published next year.

Printed in the United States
107147LV00001B/29/P

9 780979 702204